The New Pattern of Language Teaching

DAVID H. HARDING

Lecturer in Modern Language Method
Department of Education
University of Leeds

1724

LONGMANS

LONGMANS, GREEN & CO LTD
48 Grosvenor Street, London W1

© *David Harding 1967*
First published 1967

Printed in Great Britain by
Neill & Company Limited
Edinburgh

Preface

The task of the modern languages teacher is a difficult one. His subject requires that he should not only maintain mastery of his academic knowledge and of his pedagogical skill, but also that he should always be a proficient user of the foreign language in speech and writing. In addition to this, he is usually expected to be a living representative of the life and culture of a foreign nation. As far as methodology is concerned, language teaching has been so strongly debated over the last seventy or eighty years that the teacher may find himself criticised whatever 'method' he adopts. As he probably wishes to teach in the active way that exercise in the use of language requires, each day in the classroom is tiring physically and mentally. He also has a considerable load of marking, probably runs a French circle or a German club, and in the holidays takes pupils abroad.

Recent developments in modern language teaching have added a number of complications to the language teacher's life. He now often has to use audio-visual aids, such as projectors and tape-recorders, and he may be expected to teach in a language laboratory, where electronic equipment must be manipulated by him and by his class. The preparation of materials on tape for such teaching imposes an enormous amount of work, which the teacher's own training may not have equipped him to carry out. Developments in linguistics are bringing new lines of thought into his academic subject, which may bewilder rather than help him. The familiar Ordinary level language papers are showing signs of change; languages are being taught in primary schools, and to all pupils in some comprehensive schools. It is understandable if the language teacher feels a little uncertain of himself or insecure amid these many changes.

This book attempts to give a concise account of these new developments in the field of language teaching, though it is not possible in the space of one small volume to give more than an introduction to the subject. The book also attempts to relate these various developments to the changes that are taking place in the organisation of education in Britain. In new types of schools and in a new type of education, language teaching will occupy a somewhat different position from what it has done in our schools during the first half of the century. This book attempts to describe what that new position will be, and so to trace a new pattern of language teaching.

PART ONE considers the historical and theoretical background to the present situation. The first chapter is an historical review of language teaching in this country and elsewhere since the end of the last century. In the second chapter the reasons for which languages have been taught are surveyed in order to obtain a clearer view of the objective of language teaching today. Then follows a chapter on the relevance of linguistics and one on the development of the theory of language teaching.

PART TWO is concerned with current developments. It is in this part that the use of audio-visual courses, language laboratories and other new types of media are surveyed, and also present developments in testing and examining.

PART THREE outlines the effect on language teaching in schools and colleges that is being produced by the trends described in Part One and by the practical developments which are surveyed in Part Two. In the three chapters of Part Three the new shape of language teaching is considered in the three statutory levels of education in Britain: primary, secondary and further. In the final chapter on further education some reference is made to university work and the training of teachers.

The book can be regarded as a study in curriculum development. It is concerned with the teaching of a group of closely related subjects—modern languages—and it traces developments that are taking place in the content of these subjects, in the methods by which they are taught and in the place they occupy in the curriculum in schools. It is necessary in such a study to outline the various forces that determine these developments in the curriculum and to show how they fit into wider changes in the whole field of education.

It is hoped that the book will be useful to students in training, to teachers and to others interested in language teaching. As an introduction to the subject it does not assume that the reader has necessarily any experience as a language teacher himself. Practising teachers who read the book must forgive me if in certain places I explain in detail things which to them are well-known or obvious. Such matters may not be so obvious to the uninitiated. I am well aware of the imperfections of the book and of the scanty treatment that I have given to some topics, which would deserve much greater attention if space allowed. Yet this one reasonably compact survey of language teaching today will, I hope, meet a real need. I have indicated at many points in the text, in footnotes and in the bibliography, what further reading can be done to extend knowledge of the subject. It may well be, in this rapidly developing field, that, before this comes into the hands of the reader, other significant developments will have taken place. The reader will need to keep himself up to date by referring to recent issues of the language teaching periodicals listed in the bibliography.

I wish to thank the many teachers in and around Leeds whose enterprising work in language teaching has largely stimulated me to write this book and provided me with much of my material. I wish also to thank Dr H. H. Stern, of the Language Centre at the University of Essex for reading the whole manuscript and making many valuable suggestions; Mr Richard Handscombe, of the Nuffield Foreign Languages Teaching Materials Project, and Mr Michael Gregory, formerly of the School of English in Leeds University, for their invaluable advice and help in connection with Chapter 3; Mr H. S. Otter, former Director of the M.L.A. Examinations Project, for help with Chapter Seven, and for permisison to include details about his work; Dr K. Lovell, of the Leeds University Institute of Education, for advising me about certain parts of Chapter 2; and most important of all, my wife for her unfailing encouragement and for typing and retyping the manuscript.

Finally, I wish to make clear that whatever valuable help I have received from others, I have the sole responsibility for the opinions expressed in this book.

D. H. HARDING

Leeds, April 1966

Acknowledgements

We are indebted to the following for permission to reproduce copyright material:

Mr E. W. Hawkins, M.A. for material from *Modern Languages in the Grammar School*, and Methuen & Co. Ltd. for material from *A Programmed German Grammar* by A. K. Tyrer.

Contents

Part One

The Background

I

Historical Review

In order to understand the principal issues in the field of modern language teaching in the middle of the twentieth century, it is helpful briefly to review the developments of the last hundred years or so. The various views of language teaching that have been held in recent years owe a great deal to currents of thought on the subject that run back well into the last century. We find that traditional ideas linger on even when modern experience and the demands of modern life show that those ideas must of necessity be modified. This is not to say that tradition is of itself a bad thing, and indeed if we could attach ourselves to the best traditions we should find that developments which may have appeared revolutionary in the 1960s are in fact no more than the reassertion of principles that have been held for decades, if not for centuries, by those who had an insight into the true nature of language learning. Perhaps more important is the fact that while for a long time lip-service has been paid to certain principles, practice in the schools has been far removed from the kind of work that these principles demanded. In our historical review we need to see why this should be, lest history should repeat itself and the great possibilities that technology, psychology and linguistic science now offer us should never be realised in the schools.

The Nineteenth Century

Fascinating as may be the ideas of Montaigne, Comenius, Locke and others, we need go no farther back than the nineteenth century to gain a true perspective. Education a hundred

3

years ago was so dominated by the teaching of the classics, by the linguistic and literary disciplines of the ancient languages of Greece and Rome, that any study of modern or contemporary languages was relegated to a place of minor importance. The educational value of Latin and Greek was held in such unrivalled esteem that the claims of modern languages could not seriously be considered as an alternative, and the provision for the study of French or German at university level was scanty indeed. This was bad enough, but the position was made infinitely worse by the fact that the methods used in teaching the dead languages of the past were systematically applied to teaching the living languages of the present. The textbooks produced at this time were very largely influenced by the methods of the German textbook writer Karl Plötz (1819-81), whose books enjoyed a great vogue on the continent. They consisted on the one hand of a series of grammatical rules illustrated by examples and accompanied by paradigms, and, on the other hand, of a large number of exercises in which sentences in the mother tongue were to be translated into the foreign language. The method of teaching followed the textbook; it was based on grammar and translation; it paid little or no attention to the spoken language and ignored the possibilities of spontaneous learning without recourse to translation. Frequently classics masters taught a little French, and taught it as a secondary subject, but approached it with the same methods as were used in teaching Latin. French nationals were also often used to teach French, and though these men usually tried to do a bit of oral work, they were not respected, failed to keep order, and so the subject came into further disrepute.

The Clarendon Commissioners, reporting in 1864, invited the headmasters of the great public schools to form Modern Sides, which most of them did, but with some reluctance. In 1879 the Headmasters' Conference discussed the teaching of modern languages, and agreed on these principles: the study of French and German had a high value as mental gymnastics, though it was not to be thought of as quite equal to that of the classics; philosophy was a valuable subject for school study; it was impossible to teach oral French in schools. Those who most warmly advocated the study of modern languages at that time saw them as grammatical and literary studies and did not see that any benefit could result from a study of the contemporary spoken language. Though there were some teachers, particularly phoneticians, who wished to make the spoken language the centre of instruction, there were no suitable textbooks for French teaching to enable this view to be practised in the classroom.

The dominant position of Britain in the world politically and militarily during the Victorian era gave the monolingual Englishman a false sense of security. As a representative of a 'superior culture', he could usually expect the foreigner to have some knowledge of English. The Englishman abroad preferred to remain somewhat aloof from the warring factions in continental Europe; there was little or no incentive to learn the languages of Napoleon or Bismarck. At the same time the learning of a foreign language, if it had to be learned for urgent reasons, was considered something of a casual part-time task; any intelligent man could pick up a smattering if he had to, and many a colonial administrator did in fact learn something of the languages he met in India or Africa. But the learning of languages was not considered professionally or scientifically by more than a very few.

The Reform Movement

Round about 1880 and in the following years, a great change came. It was in 1882 that Viëtor published in Germany his vigorous and forthright pamphlet under the militant title, *Der Sprachunterricht muss umkehren*. He launched a full attack on the current grammar–translation method, insisting that the pupil should not be presented with rules about language, but should discover the facts for himself by experience in the language. Drawing very largely on the phoneticians Sayce and Sweet, he maintained that language must not too much be analysed into words, but taught in complete sentence utterances. Language was to be learned through speech first; even accidence was to be learned from the sounds of speech

5

rather than from written endings. Already two years earlier, Gouin's remarkable book, *L'Art d'Enseigner et d'Étudier les Langues,* had appeared in France, but this remained almost unknown until the Englishman Swan discovered it in 1889, translated it into English and published it in London. Gouin thought that a foreign language should be learned more or less as a child learns his mother tongue, and to this end he developed 'series' of actions and accompanying statements, through which the basic utterances of the language were to be acquired.

The dawn of the Direct Method had broken across Europe, and in the years following 1880 a great deal of controversy took place about the merits and demerits of the new method. In 1882 the *Société Nationale des Professeurs de Français en Angleterre* was formed, and at its first conference passed a resolution that French should be taught as a living language, and another to the effect that it should be taught by Frenchmen. In 1884 Franke in his book *Die Praktische Sprachlernung* amplified the work of Viëtor. Two years later in France, Paul Passy initiated *Le Maître Phonétique,* a monthly journal in support of the new method of language teaching. In England a conference of modern languages teachers was held in Cheltenham in 1890, organized mainly by W. H. Widgery, W. S. MacGowan and Henry Sweet. Speakers at this conference included Viëtor and Passy, and resolutions were passed that would make phonetics the basis of language teaching and the reading book the centre of instruction.

Though there were some differences of view among these Direct Methodists, we can see that in the main they were remarkably united in their outlook on language teaching. They were strongly opposed to the grammar–translation method of the day, and generally opposed to all translation into the target language. They believed in learning the language in and through the language itself, and hence did not favour the intrusion of the mother tongue in the classroom. They believed in the priority that must be given to speech and to spoken language. Many of them, like Passy and Sweet, were in any case phoneticians and favoured an extensive use of phonetics in language teaching. Grammar was to be learned inductively by the frequent use of the language, and rules were virtually banned. Meanings of words were to be learned as far as possible by the direct association of the new word with the thing or concept that it designated, without the intervention of the mother tongue. They also believed that the significant unit of language was the sentence rather than the word, and that the reading book was to be central in the language lesson, as explained by Jesperson in *How to Teach a Foreign Language.*

We would accept practically all these ideas today, though we might put a somewhat different emphasis in certain places. What these great linguists and language teachers of the end of the last century seem to have missed completely is the principle of selection, grading and controlled presentation of linguistic items, first vocabulary and then structures. They did not make word counts, nor did they arrive at the idea of a basic vocabulary; they did not scientifically grade the structures of the languages they taught for controlled and systematic presentation. In the second place, through no fault of theirs, they did not have the technological aids to language teaching that we dispose of today. These factors imposed limitations on the excellent principles they had evolved.[1]

The Direct Method in England

The new Direct or Reformed Method of teaching languages was taken up with enthusiasm by some of the finest language teachers in England at the time. W. H. Widgery, of University College School, and W. S. MacGowan, of Cheltenham College, were two men who not only practised the method in the classroom, but also laboured hard in lecturing and writing to convince other teachers of the value of the new principles. Walter Ripman set about producing the necessary textbooks

[1] More detailed information about language teaching in England at the end of the last century is given in three articles by Mark Gilbert, entitled 'The Origins of the Reform Movement in Modern Language Teaching in England', in the *Durham Research Review*, Vol. I, Nos. 4 and 5, and Vol. II, No. 6, 1953-1955.

and in collaboration with Alge produced his *First French Book* in 1898. In the early years of this century there were some able teachers, such as de Glehn, of the Leys School, Cambridge, who were undoubtedly doing excellent work in the Direct Method. As long as the teachers concerned were able and gifted men, with a true understanding of both language and the learning process, all went well. There have always been teachers who have successfully followed the best principles of language teaching ever since the remarkable developments of the 1880s.

But the new method needed to be adequately adapted to conditions in the schools, and this is where the hardest part of the task lay. Textbooks and other materials were needed for schools, detailed programmes needed to be worked out, giving a clear idea of what could and what could not be achieved in a given time at school. Teachers needed to be trained, and the method so clearly developed that it could be used by the average or less than average teacher with the average or less than average class. All this involved a tremendous task which could not be accomplished in a few years only. As time went on it became apparent that the new method in the hands of a poor teacher could be a hopeless failure. Since the active methods involved could lead to poor discipline, the new ideas earned considerable ill-repute, if not outright scorn. At the same time there must have been a large number of languages teachers who remained virtually unaffected by the innovations, or who actively resisted them. These teachers would find welcome support for their conservatism in the failures of the Reformed Method to secure examination successes.

While this confusing state of affairs was developing in practical teaching, H. E. Palmer was at work scrutinising the principles of the Direct Method on the theoretical plane. His book, *The Scientific Study and Teaching of Languages,* appeared in 1917, and in it Palmer exposed what he called the 'fallacy' of the Direct Method. He maintained that some of the means which Direct Methodists used to convey meaning were more cumbersome and confusing, in fact far less 'direct', than a simple translation into the mother tongue. To learn all meanings by

8

context, as the child learns his L1,[1] would take far too long. In any case the pupil usually guesses the English translation and repeats this to himself, so that translation does in fact take place. Far from being an opponent of the Direct Method, Palmer was enthusiastic in his support of most of the ideas of the reformers, but he sought to give them more reality, a more scientific form. He was very successful in reorganising the teaching of English in Japan along active oral lines, and did as much as anybody towards making the new method a success in practice.

The Status of Modern Languages

Side by side with this question of method was another not unrelated issue. This was the question of the emergence of modern languages as an academic subject that claimed equal status with classics. As we have seen, in the latter part of the nineteenth century Modern Sides began to develop in the great public schools. In 1886 the Modern Languages Tripos was instituted at Cambridge, but it was as late as 1903 that the Honours School of Modern Languages was set up at Oxford. By the end of the First World War there were chairs of French in most universities, with a few notable exceptions, but the total number of university staff appointments in all languages and throughout the country was no more than about 150. Modern languages as an academic subject was slowly gaining ground, but the struggle for status and recognition was an arduous one.

The new grammar schools, founded as a result of the Education Act of 1902, were not so deeply committed to classical studies as were the old endowed schools and the public schools. Consequently they were more likely to develop the teaching of modern languages. This they certainly did, though one could not say that the older schools neglected the subject. In 1918 the Leathes Committee on the position of modern languages in the educational system of Great Britain published

[1] It is now fairly generally accepted by linguists in Britain and America that the symbol L1 represents a speaker's native language, his mother tongue, and that L2 represents his first acquired language, L3 his second acquired language, and so on.

its report, *Modern Studies*. This interesting report examined the situation at that time very fully and made recommendations to promote the study of languages and their accompanying cultures. The authors of the report envisaged modern language learning as fitting clearly into the educational system, and therefore they advised that pupils should begin the study of a foreign language at the age of eleven, which was by then recognised as the age of transfer from the elementary to the secondary schools. This report definitely established the position of modern languages in both schools and universities.

In the interwar years there was an increased awareness of the need for language teaching in our schools. Many textbooks, some of them excellent, were produced and also a good selection of suitable readers in both French and German. But the Spens report, *Secondary Education*, which appeared in 1938, devoted little more than one of its 477 pages to languages in schools, though it did emphasise that 'all pupils should be given the chance of learning at least one language other than their own'.[1] The Norwood report of 1941 had one complete chapter on modern languages, in which the importance of the subject is clearly realised. 'Few would be prepared to deny,' the report states, 'the strength of the case for a more extensive knowledge of foreign languages in this country.'[2] The position of the subject had been recognised.

The Compromise Method

In the period between the two world wars a considerable body of language teachers in this country successfully adapted the Direct Method to the practical requirements of work in the schools. The more extreme ideas of some enthusiasts were avoided, while the main principle of learning through oral practice in the language, rather than through grammar and translation, was put into effective operation. F. A. Hedgcock, whose *Active French Course* appeared between 1926 and 1929,

[1] *Secondary Education;* report of the Consultative Committee (Spens report), H.M.S.O., 1938, p. 175.

[2] *Curriculum and Examinations in Secondary Schools;* report of the Committee of the Secondary Schools Examinations Council (Norwood report), H.M.S.O., 1943, p. 115.

was one of those who sought to make a form of Direct Method teaching a reality in schools. Excellent as his course was in many ways, it still made very extensive use of phonetic symbols, which would not make it acceptable to all teachers. More significant, and even more widely used, was H. F. Collins' *A French Course for Schools*, the first book of which appeared in 1929. Collins succeeded in producing a course book that was thorough and safe in the hands of any teacher, that met the requirements of school work and that provided all the linguistic material needed for active oral lessons. Writing in the *Year Book of Education*, 1934, Collins, who later became Staff Inspector in modern languages, expounded his views on method very clearly. He explained the deficiencies of the full Direct Method, the strain on the teacher, the absurdity of banning all English from the classroom, the danger of neglecting written work, and so on. He continued:

'The writer claims that a compromise method, one that does not scorn to explain a real difficulty in lucid English, but one that never loses grip of the foreign language, that uses it whenever possible and aims at pronunciation, conversation, and grammatical accuracy in written work, is a possible solution. Each lesson should aim at affording some practice in all these sections: to isolate any one must tend to destroy linguistic fabric. If we are teaching German, let us teach as Germanly as possible; let us consciously create in our classroom a German atmosphere. Let Henry become Heinrich and Mary Marie, and let them hear all class directions in the language they are trying to acquire; but let them proceed step by step under the wise guidance of a teacher who will not befog them in the name of some pedagogical shibboleth and, when passive voice and modal verbs come along, will not put them off with meaningless German explanations when clear English, in a few minutes, would make foundations secure.'[1]

In a very similar way the handbook of the Incorporated Association of Assistant Masters, which appeared in 1949 under

[1] H. F. Collins, 'Modern Languages', in *The Yearbook of Education*, 1934, p. 419.

the title *The Teaching of Modern Languages,* examined the Direct Method and found it wanting. The authors of the handbook went on:

'We therefore recommend what we prefer to call the Oral Method, rejecting the uncompromising Direct Method, but accepting most of the contentions of its advocates. Our Oral Method would insist on a maximum of oral work, varying with the form, the circumstances and the teacher, with the Year to be taught and with the previous teaching of the pupils, but always on the understanding that it is neither a method nor an academician that teaches, but a teacher. The Oral Method . . . presupposes a wholesome but difficult discipline—permitting chatter and even fooling that can be controlled at a glance, and based on a real and friendly understanding with the pupils. . . . It can well be applied, not merely to simple conversation and to classroom business, but to reading, the correction of exercises, preparation for free composition, games and the like. It will not be applied to the very necessary teaching of formal grammar.' [1]

It is not difficult to visualise the excellent teaching that went on in some schools according to this compromise or oral method. Especially in the lower years of the grammar schools some really first-class work was done. We must also recognise the tremendous achievement of Collins and those teachers who were likeminded, in successfully practising in schools the principles of the Direct Methodists adapted to the classroom situation. During those interwar years the use of the gramophone as a teaching aid was developed and the value of the recorded voice was recognised, even though the actual use of the gramophone may have been very limited. Pupil correspondence with foreign pupils, exchange visits and school journeys abroad all developed considerably, and most large schools had a French 'assistant'. In 1937 the first two books of Mrs Saxelby's remarkable course appeared, *En Route* and *En Marche*. Wherever these were adopted they brought vigour and freshness into the teaching of French. Much more than

[1] The Incorporated Association of Assistant Masters, *The Teaching of Modern Languages,* University of London Press, 1949, pp. 89, 90.

Collins's books, they used the language to give access to the life of a people at home, at work and at play. The two following volumes, *En France* and *Enfants de France,* introduced pupils to French literature, and made alive the customs, traditions and folklore of the various provinces of France.

While there was much that was good in language teaching, we must remember that before the Second World War, as also after it, there was much teaching in schools that was very inferior. Many teachers had not the capacity or the energy to teach in the manner of Collins and Mrs Saxelby. In many schools a good start was made with the Oral Method in the early years, but there was a gradual lapse into grammar and translation in the middle school. In fact the so-called Oral Method left the door wide open for this. There was no clear-cut line of distinction between the Oral Method and the old grammar–translation method. Vernon Mallinson was hardly exaggerating when he wrote:

'Once the defences were down the rot set in. It was all very well advocating a "compromise" method to retain all that was best in the Direct Method, to teach as Frenchily or as Germanly as possible, but it left the unexperienced or ill-equipped teacher floundering, returning for self-protection to the old translational method, or at the best using to the best of his ability (which usually meant slavishly) the several courses that now came on to the market in vindication of the trumpeted compromise.'[1]

And so there was wide diversity of approach and method, as the authors of the I.A.A.M. handbook clearly stated. But all the fulminations of Mallinson and others did little more than effect a minority of teachers, until, round about 1960, changes of a more radical nature began to take place. Before we go on to consider these, we will glance at what was happening across the Atlantic.

Developments in the U.S.A.
For a full account of the study and teaching of languages in the United States the reader must turn elsewhere. (*The Study*

[1] V. Mallinson, *Teaching a Modern Language,* Heinemann, 1953, p. 19.

of Language by J. B. Carroll is a good introduction, but needs to be supplemented by more recent books such as Lado: *Language Teaching* and Rivers: *The Psychologist and the Foreign Language Teacher*.) Here we intend to give only some broad indication of significant developments insofar as they affect our understanding of the present situation in this country.

In the years before the Second World War there developed in America a method of teaching languages known as the reading method. Remoteness from Europe and, in many cases, lack of motivation made it very difficult to expect American pupils to acquire a competent knowledge of the spoken language. But readers and simplified versions of literary works were available, so that pupils could both learn through reading and profit educationally from the ability to read elementary works of French or German literature. This method has received some very strong criticism, and it is true to say that a good deal of language teaching in American schools was ineffective and inefficient.

If language teaching itself was at this time in the doldrums, there were nevertheless significant developments related to language teaching that were taking place in the United States. Partly under the influence of behaviourist psychology, a number of word frequency counts were made in the interwar years. Notable here was the work of the psychologist Thorndike, who counted the relative frequency of words in English texts for the purpose of assisting the teaching of reading. Work on word counts implied the principle that linguistic material needed to be both limited and graded for teaching purposes. This was a great advance, as these were ideas that seem to have been largely absent from the thinking of the European Direct Methodists. In addition to this, the scientific study of linguistics was growing in America under the influence of the two great linguists of this period: Edward Sapir and Leonard Bloomfield. The study of American Indian languages was a very fruitful field for these men and their students. Bloomfield was able to blend this new work on the description of exotic languages with the traditions of European philology, and to maintain at the same time a respect for a behaviourist approach to language. His book, *Language,* which appeared in 1933, is a scholarly statement on language which formed a basis for linguistic work that was to follow.

It should be said here that the U.S.A. was not the only country in which linguistic science was developing, and interesting work was being done in England and on the continent of Europe. C. K. Ogden, for example, produced Basic English, which was described in a book published in 1930. Basic English is restricted to a vocabulary of 850 words, which can be used to express almost any idea. The other words of normal English are replaced in Basic by definitions that use only the limited vocabulary. The criterion for selecting these 850 words was not frequency, but the capacity to cover, in various combinations, all possible lexical functions. Basic was thus an attempt to restrict English in such a way as to make the language much easier to learn without reducing its usefulness.

While Bloomfield and other linguists were impatient with much of the conventional school language teaching of their day, they could do hardly anything to influence classroom practice directly. However, the urgent need for rapid and efficient language teaching in the U.S. forces that arose in the Second World War highlighted the fact that these conventional methods were totally inadequate, and it also provided opportunities in which linguists could have some influence at least on language teaching. Early in 1941, before the United States even entered the war, the American Council of Learned Societies established an Intensive Language Program for studying several unusual languages and for providing materials for teaching them. This work resulted in an intensive language teaching course at the University of Michigan, where a linguistic scientist actually directed the classroom teaching process. Among various other projects of language teaching, the Army Specialised Training Program was perhaps the most extensive and gained considerable publicity. Various languages, including French and German, as well as more unusual ones, were studied intensively, generally for a nine months period, by Army personnel. The emphasis was on the spoken word and the colloquial language. Methods varied widely but usually included intensive oral work. Linguistic scientists were in charge of this work in only a few cases, but the general influence of linguistic theory may have been felt more widely. These ASTP courses were remarkably successful and surprised educators who were accustomed to the poor results and low oral standards of traditional high school and college language teaching.

After the war attempts were made to introduce the methods of the ASTP into school language work. This could never be fully achieved, as in school a foreign language is one of several subjects, whereas in the Army courses it was the almost exclusive concern of the students for the duration of the course. But the stimulus to school language teaching was a wholesome one, and ultimately some real progress was made. Language laboratories and audio-lingual courses came to be accepted as essential to language teaching in schools several years before they were seriously considered in Britain. A project of foreign language teaching in elementary schools was launched in the 1950s, which we shall consider in more detail in Chapter 8. The National Defense Education Act of 1958 allocated funds specifically for language teaching, amongst other educational matters, and thus the need for improving the nation's language learning was officially recognised and considered. Meanwhile linguistic science had been making steady progress, especially in certain centres, such as the English Language Institute of the University of Michigan. But this is a subject to which we shall return in our chapter on linguistics.

The Postwar Period

In Britain the new secondary education that was established by the Act of 1944 offered possibilities for a great extension of modern language teaching in schools. Not only was grammar school education greatly extended and developed, which meant that increasing numbers of pupils learned a foreign language in a grammar school, but also many secondary modern schools began to teach French to their A streams, and sometimes to B or C streams as well. The numbers of pupils taking a foreign language at Ordinary level in the new G.C.E. examination showed a steady increase. At the same time many of the pupils learning a language in secondary modern or comprehensive schools could not hope to reach the academic standard of Ordinary level, and a good deal of thought was given to the needs of these pupils and the methods by which they should be taught. Evelyn Coulson's book, *French in the Secondary School* (1947), showed how such teaching could be approached, and the subject was further considered by a committee of the Modern Languages Association a few years later.

The postwar years also saw new course books appearing on the market at the rate of two or three completely new courses almost every year. Some of these are very good indeed. All accept the general conception of the Oral Method, with varying degrees of emphasis on conversational or written work. Here and there really original ideas on details of method are to be found in these books. Not only French courses appeared, but also new courses in German, Spanish and, more recently, Russian. But it was clear that the general pattern of language teaching established in the earlier years of the century was continuing basically unchanged. Some teaching was very good, in fact beyond any criticism. At the same time a good deal of work had fallen back to dull and unsatisfactory methods.

In the late 1950s and early 1960s changes burst upon the language teaching scene in Britain and elsewhere, which can be seen as analogous to the stirring developments of the 1880s. While the birth of the Direct Method was due in large measure to the growth of the academic study of phonetics, the equally far reaching developments of recent times can trace their origin to the threefold source of technology, psychology and linguistics. These are the areas of scientific knowledge that lie behind, and influence, current trends. First, electronic means of recording the human voice on magnetic tape, which have been developed in the last twenty years or so, have largely superseded the gramophone and led to the widespread use of tape-recorders and ultimately to the development of the language laboratory. Visual projection now offers us a range of possibilities, including slides, film-strips, cine-films and film loops, all of which can play some part in language teaching, now that projectors are produced that can be easily handled in the classroom. All this is the contribution of technology. Secondly, we have already seen that the work of behaviourist psychologists led to word frequency counts, which was a notable contribution to language teaching. Other aspects of language learning have also been influenced by psychology. For example, the comparative ease with which young children can learn a foreign language orally has been shown to have a basis in the psychology of the child. Thirdly, the academic and scientific study of linguistics has contributed a far better knowledge of the structure of language and how it operates. Extensive linguistic studies have also been undertaken to aid language learning. The production of Basic English was one such study. Even more significant has been the work of French linguists in developing *Le Français Fondamental*. This is not a restricted language complete in itself, as Basic English. It is simply the essential elements of French lexis and grammar which need to be mastered before the technical or literary language is studied. This is an example of the assistance that linguistics is giving to language teaching.

These developments have come at a time when language teaching is becoming increasingly important throughout the world. There is an enormous demand for English and French teaching in the developing countries of Africa, just as there is a great need for Russian in certain other parts of the world.

The idealistic view that one master-key language, whether it be Esperanto, Basic English or any other, could perhaps solve the language problems of the world, has had to give way before the resurgence of nationalism and national languages that is raising an increasing number of languages to a level of international importance. Chinese, Arabic, Swahili and Urdu are becoming as important as European tongues. Nearer home we find that the countries of Western Europe are endeavouring to draw closer to one another, and Britain's commercial and economic links with the rest of Europe are stronger than ever before. British industry is crying out for personnel skilled in one or more European languages in addition to English.

Practically, these factors have produced in our schools a number of developments in language teaching which have affected most language teachers in some form or other. It is the aim of this book to describe these new developments in some detail, to assess as far as possible their importance in the present educational scene and to trace the new pattern of language teaching which appears to be emerging in this country.

2

Reasons for Teaching Languages

Throughout the period that we have surveyed the reasons for language teaching in Britain have varied considerably. A complex of social, economic, educational and cultural reasons may underlie the teaching of a particular language at a given place and time. At different places and in different times the reasons will vary, or different emphases will be put within the complex of reasons. An Australian high school boy learning French will be motivated by reasons which differ considerably from those of a Nigerian youngster learning English. And yet in these two extreme cases some of the reasons will overlap. The reasons for teaching a language influence our whole approach to the language and the methods by which we teach it. It is necessary therefore at this point to consider our reasons and to notice the shift in emphasis that has taken place over the years. Reasons for teaching languages in British schools today are significantly different from what they were at the close of the last century.

The Key to a Culture

In the time of the Roman empire, Latin was the lingua franca of Western Europe; it was used for everyday communication, both oral and written, and was learned for this purpose. During the Dark Ages, and on to the time of the Renaissance, Latin retained some of its importance as an international language for communication. But gradually it lost ground in this respect, and national languages took on a far greater significance. There was no point in Victorian England in learning Latin if one's sole objective was to communicate with foreign people. Another powerful reason for learning Latin had arisen. Latin was the key to the culture of the ancient world, for in that language the great works of Roman literature and learning were written. This literature was still of immense significance, and to read it the scholar had to be well acquainted with Latin. Such acquaintance had to be with the written or literary language, not with the language as it had once lived on the lips of Roman citizens. Indeed conversational Latin had been largely lost. The nineteenth-century schoolboy was taught a written language, and it mattered not at all if he could not speak the language he read and studied. A change in reason for learning involved a change in method of learning, a different approach to the language.

When, as we have seen in our first chapter, modern languages came to be taught in our schools, they were at first taught in much the same way as Latin, with little reference to the spoken word. This was because the reason for learning these modern languages was also a literary one. French was learned as the language of Corneille and Molière, of Voltaire and Diderot; it was in fact a key to a culture. French does indeed enshrine a great literary heritage, and so do English, German, Spanish, Italian and Russian. If modern languages were to hold a place in the curriculum that could be considered equal in its cultural and educative value to that of the classics, then it had to be shown that these languages opened the way to a first-hand understanding of foreign literatures, and that these literatures were of intrinsic cultural value. It was almost inevitable that French and German and other languages should be taught with this objective, and the study of literary texts became part of modern languages courses in secondary schools.

The study of the great works of French and German literature has in fact become in Britain an academic pursuit of high prestige. 'Modern Languages' as a sixth-form and university subject makes very considerable demands on those who study it. Modern linguists have had to struggle for a place in the academic world, and they have won that place rightly and deservedly. To read and like reading Racine, to appreciate

Sartre or Proust, to have embraced the wisdom of Goethe, or reached an understanding of Kafka, these are achievements which involve for English-speaking readers many years of linguistic and literary study. This literary prestige, however, has tended to obscure the fact that literature is but one of the ways in which language is used. There are other types of acquaintance with a language, which may have nothing to do with literary studies. French is used by literary authors, but it is also used by engineers and mechanics, by technicians and labourers, by shopkeepers and busdrivers, by men and women in factories and offices and in every other walk of life.

Many teachers, particularly at university level, would maintain that to provide access to the literature is the main objective of language teaching. They would argue that language is the means of communication that poets, dramatists, novelists, historians and philosophers have used for greater ends. To give students some mastery of the means without leading them to the ends is pointless; it merely makes them articulate and verbal, without giving them anything to say. The real value of learning a modern language, it is maintained, lies in the study of literature. At the same time it has been realized that it is quite unreal to divorce the literary language from the language of everyday life. The more teachers have introduced their pupils to the works of contemporary writers, the more it has been realised that to study a modern language in the way that Latin has been studied is to miss half the understanding of that modern language's literature. Only by understanding the force, the colour and the overtones of words and phrases in everyday conversation can readers come to see the importance of those expressions when employed by a successful writer in poetry, in drama or in the novel. In any case most poetry is meant to be spoken, and most drama is essentially a literary use of spoken language. The novel, too, is often full of dialogue, which presupposes in the reader the ability to imagine mentally what the cut-and-thrust of language in everyday speech would be. The literary reason for learning languages does not then justify any neglect of the spoken language.

As the twentieth century has progressed, the teaching of foreign literatures has become more and more linked with the spoken language of today. As increasing attention has been given to the works of contemporary authors in sixth-form and university courses, so the study of literature and the study of the contemporary spoken language have come closer together. However, the great increase in numbers of pupils in grammar schools since 1900 and the growth of scientific studies at sixth-form level have meant that a very small proportion of pupils learning a foreign language in secondary schools do in fact proceed to read the literature written in that language. Yet French is widely taught to thousands of pupils who are never likely to know much more of French literature than the occasional fable of La Fontaine, learned at school. As the trend of expansion continues and French is taught in secondary modern and comprehensive schools, there must be reasons other than the literary one for continuing to teach it.

Educational Reasons

Classical languages were taught in Victorian schools, not only because they led to a cultural heritage, but also because it was believed that the academic work involved in mastering Latin and Greek was a valuable discipline for the mind. In order to establish modern languages in our schools it had to be shown that French and German could provide just as much academic discipline as the classical languages, though this has been hotly disputed and some might not accept it even today. Even when direct comparison with the classics was no longer necessary, it was found that there were cogent educational reasons for including French, German and other modern languages in the curriculum. As a school subject a foreign language is, like mathematics, cumulative; that is to say, the pupil is constantly building on work that has gone before. In the descriptive sciences or in geography or history, it may be possible to start a fresh topic at the beginning of a new term and do well at it, even though work done in the previous term has been very imperfectly understood. Not so in languages; here it is very clear that a shaky foundation will never support a firm edifice.

A modern language is, then, a demanding subject education-ally, and success in it is proof of a certain kind of ability. This is particularly so in learning to write in the language, since grammatical accuracy in writing demands an understanding of the finer aspects of agreement, of the use of tenses, and other similarly difficult points. It is the ability to use the written language that can most accurately and most easily be tested by the type of examination that has been used now for about a hundred years. The whole system of examining candidates in various subjects in the G.C.E. examinations is to a large extent respected and trusted by employers in industry, by the civil service, by professional bodies and by universities. This respect and trust is well justified, for the examinations are on the whole reliable tests. As far as modern languages are concerned it is generally accepted that only candidates with a certain level of general intelligence and with a certain capacity for thought-ful work can achieve an Ordinary level pass. The fact that the examination in a modern language present a task of real intellectual difficulty is shown by frequest cases of boys or girls who have done quite adequate work in the sixth form in some other subjects, but yet have achieved Ordinary level French only with the greatest of difficulty after repeated attempts to pass the examination. We shall have more to say in Chapter 7 about the nature of these examinations and about what they really do test.

This educational hurdle becomes the main objective for many pupils, and for a good many teachers too. Teachers rightly feel a certain responsibility to get their pupils through an examination that may be vital for them in their careers. But since this is an examination in the written language very largely, this has led to a proportionately large emphasis on written work, in the period before the examination at any rate. Modern languages have become a convenient tool for testing the intellectual capacity of the pupils.

Transfer of Training

Underlying the idea of the educational value of learning a language is the whole question of transfer of training. Those who have sought to justify the heavy emphasis on grammar and translation that frequently characterises the course leading to Ordinary level in a modern language, have resorted to the argument that this work is good for the pupil's mind. It has been said that work on the grammar of written French gives training in thinking precisely, or that learning a foreign language 'helps their English'. There may be some truth in statements such as these, but we must remember that psychologists have rejected the old faulty psychology of the nineteenth century on which the older notion of transfer of training rested. It was thought at that time that the mind consisted of certain faculties such as memory, reason, imagination, and will, and that each of these faculties had to be trained by means of some discipline. It was thought that the learning of Latin and Greek trained these faculties, and that a person who had studied the classics would be well trained for any kind of mental activity, such as, for example, administering a colonial territory. These ideas, as then held, have been largely disproved. Transfer does not automatically take place, and therefore we cannot assume that the learning of a language will necessarily benefit the pupil in other mental activities.

Psychologists have, however, concluded from experiments that in certain circumstances transfer does take place. Thorndike claimed that there is some transfer from one activity to another when there are 'identical elements' in the two activities.[1] A pupil who has studied Latin will be at some advantage when he starts German, because he will know what is meant by the genitive and dative cases, for example. Anyone who has learned a modern European language will have some idea of how to tackle a second modern language of a similar kind; he will know that genders of nouns have to be learned, that adjectives will probably agree, that tenses may be simple or continuous, and so on. Beyond this it is not proved that learning a language provides any particular facility for learning any other

[1] The educational importance of transfer of training can be further studied in books on educational psychology. In particular the reader is referred to the relevant sections of these two works: Lovell, K., *Educational Psychology and Children* (U.L.P.), Chapter 10; Wall, W. D., *Education and Mental Health* (Harrap), Appendix 1C.

language; it does not train a faculty of language learning. Nor does it necessarily teach accuracy or precision. But the experience of language learning can teach a great deal about language and how it operates, especially if intelligent generalisations are made in the course of the studying. For example, by studying a foreign language one comes to realize more clearly than would otherwise be possible, that one cannot translate from one language to another by a simple transposition of word-for-word equivalents. Through learning a language one can also become more aware of the fact that, not only does a foreign language consist of different sounds and different words, but that it employs different intonation patterns. 'It is likely, for example,' writes David Abercrombie, 'that English assertions concerning the excitability of Frenchmen are founded on the fact that certain features of the speech of normal Frenchmen are closely similar to features of excitable Englishmen's speech. Americans, again, often accuse Englishmen of superciliousness: normal English intonation closely resembles the intonation adopted by supercilious Americans.'[1] The experience of learning a foreign language helps the pupil towards a just appreciation of the nature of language and of how it operates; this in turn will help him to make truer judgments in those parts of human experience that depend on language.

When psychologists modified the old idea of faculty training it was necessary also to make some reassessment of the value of language learning. Some relics of the older ideas still persist in the minds of teachers and others, but generally speaking it is not now seriously maintained that language learning 'trains the mind'. Other reasons predominate, and whatever transfer of training there may be is a subtle matter of understanding the nature of language and speech.

Understanding a People

The educational value of language learning is not limited to the literary and linguistic experiences that it offers to the pupil. Through the learning of a language pupils can be made

[1] D. Abercrombie, *Problems and Principles*, Longmans, 1956, p. 5.

acquainted with the everyday life of another people. They can be prepared for the experience of foreign travel and given some appreciation of the fascinating variety and interest that another country can offer. This can be a challenge to the assumptions implicit in the pupils' own national environment. It can open perspectives for him that he would not otherwise have seen. It can encourage understanding, toleration and sympathy towards peoples whose way of life may be different from our own.

This century, which has seen the greatest international catastrophes, has also been the time of the greatest endeavours to achieve understanding and co-operation between different nationalities and different language groups. There is no doubt that the widespread teaching of languages in schools, colleges and universities in Britain is in line with the movement away from the national isolation of the last century towards co-operation in every aspect of the international scene. As language teaching was gradually extended to a far wider range of pupils in the new grammar schools, in secondary modern schools, in comprehensive schools and even in primary schools, it was quite clear that only a small minority of these pupils were expected eventually to read foreign literatures in the original, and only some of them would do the rigorous type of linguistic work that could be compared with the academic study of Latin grammar and composition. For the majority French and German were to be taught as languages that provided access to a nearby foreign nation. Course books in these languages that have appeared since the early years of this century have introduced more and more material about life in the foreign country. Penfriendships and exchange visits have been encouraged, and school travel abroad has, since the interwar years, grown to enormous proportions. We may with some justification have doubts about how much can be learned of a foreign nation by large groups of schoolchildren herded abroad on conducted tours. But the trend indicates one of the aims underlying language teaching, and, at their best, well organised educational school journeys have been very fruitful.

Undoubtedly, the full understanding of the life of a foreign nation is a most demanding undertaking. We have here an activity that will stretch the ablest pupil to the limits of his ability, and yet which offers possibilities to all. Much of the lexis and idiom of the language will be in fact an embodiment of a nation's way of life or of the social, economic and geographic conditions in which it lives. There may, however, at times be a tendency to be drawn away from the hard realities of everyday life and work towards the more picturesque and exotic attractions of folklore or of unusual ceremonies and festivities. What is called understanding a foreign people is not then so much of a reality as it was intended to be. A good deal of study of a foreign country can also be done without using or learning the language concerned. Such study may tend to lead us away from the language itself and may have nothing much to do with the fundamental business of language learning. A skilful teacher can, however, make extensive use of material about the foreign country to provide the subject matter for his language course.

Economic Factors

These cultural and educational reasons for learning a foreign language are not to be underrated. But there are other reasons of a most important kind. The great amount of liberty that schools and other educational establishments enjoy in Britain in framing their curriculum, may keep us somewhat ignorant of the power and importance of commercial and economic factors, that are bound ultimately to have a deep effect on the teaching of languages. We cannot close our eyes to the fact that industry and commerce are crying out for more personnel capable of speaking foreign languages. The requirements of the industrial and business world, on which our national economy depends, must ultimately be heeded by schools and universities, as they have already been by technical colleges and colleges of technology.

These requirements are not simply for highly skilled professional translators and interpreters, but for men and women at all levels of industry who are capable of using a foreign language in the course of their work.

All over the world there has been a tremendous increase

since the end of World War II in the demand for foreign language teaching. The emergent countries of Africa and Asia have an enormous need for teachers of English and French. The teaching of English overseas has become something of a profession, almost an industry, of its own. Linked with this are the various activities of the British Council and the work of training establishments in English universities for teachers of English as a second language. But the increase in the demand for language teaching is not confined to overseas countries. In Britain technical and commercial colleges have been flooded with company directors, sales representatives and other executives who urgently need a working knowledge of one language or another for their work, while a number of large firms have established their own language courses for their staff.

Two reports by working parties set up by the Federation (now Confederation) of British Industries make clear what the requirements of the industrial world are in relation to languages. The first of these, *Foreign Languages in Industry*, published in 1962, quotes figures to show a proportionate increase in the trade of the United Kingdom with Western Europe since the prewar years, a trend which, it is said, may be expected to increase irrespective of whether Britain enters the European Economic Community or not. This alone indicates an increasing need for staff who have a working knowledge of European languages, but, farther afield, trade with the newer nations is on the increase, and competence in Slavonic, oriental and possibly African languages may soon be required more extensively. Requirements range from those of sales staff and overseas agents to those of secretaries and telephonists.

'There are many occasions,' the report states, 'when a high proficiency in the knowledge of a language is required on the part of both senior technical and commercial staff. Broadcasting, for instance, constitutes an outlet of increasing importance. The most usual requirement, however, is one of effective oral communication. Industry needs many more people who can speak at least one foreign language—not necessarily perfectly—provided they can do it uninhibitedly.

A large active vocabulary is more important than an accurate knowledge of grammatical detail which stops short at the point where conversation can be held. The technical man, whether concerned with sales or not, needs to have an adequate knowledge of the country or countries with which he is concerned. A man who can make himself understood in his own subject with the aid of diagrams, drawings and models, and 2,000-3,000 words in the other man's language is a valuable member of a company's staff.'[1]

These considerations lead the working party to insist further on the need for oral proficiency. They comment very favourably on the development of language teaching in primary schools, when a purely oral approach is used. They also advocate a language proficiency test of Advanced level standard, but without any literary bias, and 'concentrating on the ability to speak, read and write the foreign language with a reasonable degree of fluency'.[2] They favour the inclusion of a modern language in courses leading to higher awards in business studies, and they consider that the value of short intensive courses deserves closer consideration. The predominance of French teaching, and the comparative neglect of German and Spanish, causes them considerable concern. Finally, they support the view of the Hayter Committee that a national institute of languages should be established in Britain.

The Ministry of Education Circular 2/64, of 2 March 1964, endorsed the views of the F.B.I. working party in these terms: 'The Minister accepts the view that a large improvement in the standards of proficiency in foreign languages is needed in this country for many reasons, one of the most important being the need to maintain Britain's competitive position in world trade.'[3] In the same year another working party of the F.B.I. issued a report, *Foreign Language Needs of Industry*, which confirmed the recommendations of the earlier report and

[1] F.B.I. report, *Foreign Languages in Industry*, 1962, paragraphs 15 and 16.

[2] Ibid., p. 26.

[3] Quoted in full in F.B.I. report, *Foreign Language Needs of Industry*, 1964, pp. 45-9.

added to them. Replies to a questionnaire that had been sent to member firms of the Federation are analysed in this report. 'The demand was predominantly for oral skills for senior and sales staff and a somewhat smaller demand for written skills for technical and commercial correspondence.'[1] Again the need for oral fluency was underlined throughout the report. Language laboratories, vocabulary control and crash courses were all thought to have some contribution to make to better teaching, and changes were suggested in examinations. While much of this report is concerned with further and technical education, one recommendation is clearly aimed at schools as well: 'The educational system as a whole should provide more effectively for the training of many more young people capable of using with confidence in practical situations at least one, and in many cases two or three foreign languages, of developing their skills to a high level when required, and of learning to speak and use new languages as the need arises.'[2]   *AIMS*

Official concern about language teaching and the national need in this respect are also evidenced in the fact that in October, 1964, the Secretary of State for Education and Science and the Secretary of State for Scotland, in association with the trustees of the Nuffield Foundation, set up the Committee for Research and Development in Modern Languages. This committee, whose chairman is Mr L. Farrar-Brown, former director of the Nuffield Foundation, has ten members, who are leading educationalists, linguists and teachers, and it may be expected to play an important part in guiding developments in linguistic research and language teaching.

Language teaching is not purely an educational activity. It is of importance to industry and has become a concern to national governments. These economic and national factors are among the reasons why languages are taught in Britain, and they have become vastly more important in the last ten or twenty years. Just as the requirements of World War II gave enormous impetus to the development of audio-lingual methods in America, so the requirements of industry and

[1] Ibid., p. 5.
[2] Ibid., p. 2.

commerce are now influencing language teaching in Europe and elsewhere. The demand is mainly for persons with an effective command of the spoken language, and this is having considerable effect on how languages are taught.

The Need to Communicate   *Motivation.*

The extension of language teaching to less able pupils, doubts about the old conception of transfer of training, closer links with other language communities, the demands of industry and commerce and the changing sociological and philosophical background of education have all contributed to the formation of fresh objectives for language teaching. When a working party of the Lancashire and Cheshire Branch of the I.A.H.M. studied the problems of modern language teaching in grammar schools in 1961, the question of aims was seen to be a vital one. It is interesting to quote from the revised edition of the report that resulted from these deliberations:

> 'In attempting to cut through the tangle of confusion about aims and purposes in modern language teaching the Working Party found a helpful analogy on our own doorstep, in the bilingual areas of Wales. Why is it that the child from the Welsh valley brought up to speak Welsh at home, learns English in school? Is it to train his mind in habits of accuracy? or perhaps to foster international understanding? or to enable him to explore Shakespeare or the English novel? That this last object is frequently achieved many a Welshman both famous and obscure would testify, but what was the immediate aim in view when the first steps in English were taken in his village school? It was surely the simple aim of overcoming the barrier to communication set up by the existence of the foreign language, English. As soon as the Welsh child ventures out of his house or leaves his valley he discovers new neighbours who do not speak his mother tongue but with whom he wishes *to communicate*.
>
> 'We would not claim that the situation is precisely the same when the English child learns French. But it seemed to the Working Party that the analogy is a useful one. Our

nearest neighbours do not speak English; we are impelled partly by self-interest, partly by sheer curiosity, to communicate with them, though for the past century political and commercial events have conspired to obscure this simple truth. It is true that the challenge to the Welsh child is starker and more crudely obvious. He must learn English or suffer immediately obvious personal handicap. The English child's "motivation" is less direct, nor does one single language stand out as an essential part of his equipment for life. But the challenge is there none-the-less and the facts of living in a polyglot world community are becoming clearer to most of us.' [1]

The report goes on to explain that other reasons for language teaching certainly exist and have some importance, but the major consideration was seen to be the need to communicate. This is the basic reason why anybody learns a foreign language. Wherever, in the course of human history, different language communities have been in contact through proximity, or trade, or social and cultural exchanges, somebody has had to learn the language of the other community. The need to communicate is firstly the need to communicate in speech—to understand the speech of the foreigner and to express onself in speaking to him. As Britain for many reasons is moving closer to Europe, that need is now greater than ever before. Fewer and fewer of our young people can say with any assurance that they will never need to communicate with Frenchmen or Germans. More and more English people are travelling in Western Europe for pleasure, and holidays in Switzerland are no longer the preserve of the upper classes. One by one, features of life in continental Europe are being accepted in Britain—the twenty-four hour clock in railway timetables, international road traffic signs, a decimal coinage. As we become more and more associated with Europe, proficiency in communicating in other languages may almost become essential for national survival.

[1] I.A.H.M. (Division 12), *Modern Languages in the Grammar School,* rev. edn., 1966, p. 12.

< Teach oral German.

3

The Relevance of Linguistics

The movement in favour of teaching language as a means of oral communication has brought into greater prominence the study of linguistics. We have already seen that important developments in the field of language study have taken place in this century in both Europe and America. Linguistics has concerned itself increasingly with contemporary language, with language as it is, rather than with language as it has been, or as it ought to be. Linguistics has also concerned itself very much with spoken language, and, therefore, as language teachers have turned more to the teaching of contemporary spoken language, linguistics has become more relevant to their work. It is impossible here to give an adequate summary of the whole discipline of linguistics, but since the subject has already had an appreciable influence on those developments in language teaching which are the main theme of this book, it is necessary to give some account of what this influence is and of ways in which linguistics can be of assistance to teachers today.

What is Linguistics?
Linguistics can be described as the scientific study of language. It includes studies which are descriptions of one particular language or even of one particular part of a language. It may involve a study of a group of languages, as for example the Slavonic group or the Romance group. Or it may be concerned with language in general. As the linguist is concerned with all

aspects of language the subject embraces different types of linguistic study. Central to the subject, in the opinion of some linguists, are what may be called *lexicology* and *grammar*. The first of these is the study of words and word combinations that can be regarded as single lexical items. Grammar is concerned with the form of a stretch of language and therefore includes the study of syntactical structures and morphological systems. Lexicology can be extended to the study of the meanings of words, and to the study of meaning in general, known as *semantics*, though some linguists in the past have preferred to regard meaning as of far less importance than form. Moving away from the study of words in another direction, we come to the study of the sounds of language. This is *phonetics*, which is often considered to be a discipline distinct from linguistics, a kind of sister science. The organisation of phonetic items into groups that carry meaning is studied under *phonology*, a subject that some British linguists consider to be a bridge between the raw material of language and its formal patterning in one particular language.

In the course of the nineteenth century some most extensive and scholarly studies of European languages were produced which were of a comparative historical kind. These studies, often referred to as *philology*, are to be regarded as within the field of linguistics in its widest sense; indeed for some linguists the terms *philology* and *linguistics* are still interchangeable. More recently linguists have concentrated their attention more on contemporary languages, without reference to their historical development. Whereas nineteenth-century linguists worked mainly on data supplied by written texts, there has recently been a much greater preoccupation with spoken language, and in this work modern methods of recording speech have greatly assisted. This means that modern linguistics is much nearer to the work of the teacher of a contemporary language than was the philology of the last century.

Linguistics is a science and adopts scientific methods of procedure. It can hardly be called a physical science because language, the object of its study, is not purely physical. Various aspects of language cannot be measured with the same precision that purely physical phenomena can. As language is an element of human behaviour, linguistics can with some justice be regarded as one of the social or behavioural sciences. It is more akin to psychology or anthropology than it is to physics or chemistry. In saying that linguistics is a science we mean that it examines a body of material, namely language, and as far as possible makes an objective and exhaustive study of this material; it draws its conclusions from the evidence of the data, and does not neglect relevant facts. We mean also that it aims at consistency between all statements made about language, and prefers to make these statements in the most concise way consistent with the data.

One of the principal functions of linguistics is the *description* of languages. The data which provides the basis for the description of a language is, in theory at least, every manifestation of that language in speech or writing. In practice linguists have to limit their data to a given body of writing or recorded speech, which may in any case assume vast proportions. This data has then to be analysed, classified and described under general headings such as grammar, lexis, phonetics, and so on. In the past many, but not all, descriptions of languages have been partial, covering only some aspects of the language concerned, or they have been slanted by the desire to influence usage or by the attempt to describe one language (e.g. English) in terms appropriate only to another (e.g. Latin).

As a science linguistics has its own terminology; the linguist must be free to use the terms that are appropriate to language as he finds it to be. He cannot be satisfied with a terminology that is ambiguous or inadequate, and he must have a term for every phenomenon of language that he meets. If a suitable term does not exist, he is compelled to invent one. We should not be surprised that in the first half of the twentieth century linguists started to use terms that were unknown a hundred years ago. Terms such as *phoneme* and *morpheme,* to quote only two examples, result from the need to identify certain observable phenomena which could not be efficiently studied unless they were precisely named. Once we accept that linguistics is a science, we must also accept that it is to be dealt with by scholars who will use their own terminology. The layman cannot expect to understand at once all that linguists say, simply on the grounds that he uses language, any more than he can expect to understand at once all that psychologists say, simply on the grounds that he has a mind.[1]

Linguistics and Language Teaching

Anyone who aspires to teach a language systematically is obliged to make some study of the language he intends to teach. The ability to speak a language effectively, though essential for the language teacher, is not alone sufficient. The teacher must be able also to explain how the language operates, to state the rules that govern its grammar, to classify its various forms and to give some description of its phonetics. In undertaking this study of a language, the future teacher draws very largely on the work of the grammarians, the phoneticians and others, who have themselves studied and described various aspects of the language or languages in question. In other words, he studies linguistics, even though he may not be studying some of the most recent work in the subject.

Writers of textbooks for language teaching and authors of audio-visual language courses and of language laboratory programmes require not only a knowledge of one particular language, but also some general theory of language, some conception of the principles that underlie language and its use. It would be possible for a teacher or a course writer, although he had an excellent knowledge of the language with which he was dealing, to design an ineffective course because of a faulty appreciation of the principles by which language operates. The elements of general linguistics are an essential basis for language teaching, and for the construction of language courses.

In addition it has been found that *comparative linguistics* can be extremely valuable to the teacher and the course writer.

---

[1] An excellent account of the scientific nature of linguistics is given in R. H. Robins, *General Linguistics: An Introductory Survey*, Longmans, 1964, pp. 7-11.

Difficulties in language learning frequently concern those aspects of the target language that are markedly dissimilar from those of the learner's L1. The teacher then needs to concentrate on structures or other linguistic features that are quite different from those of the language that the learner already knows. He will try to avoid the *interference* that leads the English learner of French, for example, to say *Je le veux venir*, for *Je veux qu'il vienne*. For the teaching of western European languages in Britain most of the points where interference can arise have been discovered empirically and are suitably dealt with in courses. But in teaching English or French in Africa or Asia, or in teaching African or Asian languages in Britain, a contrastive analysis of the two languages involved would form a valuable basis for the teacher's work.

Language teachers who have mastered one or more foreign languages and who have acquired an adequate means of describing the essential features of these languages to their pupils, may find it difficult to understand how any recent advance in linguistics is of any value to them. If a teacher finds that a system of description and a terminology that he had learned from traditional textbooks is perfectly adequate for his purposes, he may see no reason why he should look any further. Modern linguistics often appears to make more complications, rather than to simplify language study. Now if a system of grammatical description is adequately effective there are certainly good reasons for retaining it. But as linguistic science advances some notions that have proved adequate for many years may be shown to be lacking. New studies of language may provide more efficient or more economic ways of describing or categorising language.

Further help for language teaching has been provided by a systematic approach to *limitation* and *grading*.[1] Limitation has been described as the process of arriving at an inventory of teaching items. Usually the teacher does not aim at teaching the whole of any one language. He omits, for example,

[1] These terms are used here, and elsewhere in this book, in the sense in which they are used and defined by M. A. K. Halliday, A. McIntosh and P. Strevens in *The Linguistic Sciences and Language Teaching*, Longmans, 1964, pp. 201-12.

thousands of technical terms and thousands of dialect forms. He may wish to teach only the spoken language of the home and the street, or he may wish to teach only the language of commercial correspondence. We have already seen that word frequency counts, as well as the production of Basic English and *Le Français Fondamental,* implied that linguistic material needed to be limited for teaching purposes. This is *limitation,* and it must operate in all successful language teaching. It will be more effective if based on a scientific study of the language. *Grading* is the process of putting these limited linguistic items in the most appropriate order for teaching purposes. It is clear that we should teach the present tense before attempting the past. Other aspects of grading may not be so self-evident. For example, a good deal of the spoken language should usually be taught before the written language is attempted. Limitation and grading are very clearly part of applied linguistics, that is, the study of language applied to language teaching.

Spoken Language

For many years the teaching of languages in Britain has been largely governed by the grammar of written language. This is partly because of the influence of the teaching of the classics, partly because of the literary objectives of language teaching, and partly because the spoken language has not been considered so valuable an object of study as the written language. It has also been implied in much that is done in language teaching that the written language, especially as it is used by the creative literary writers, is a kind of ideal towards which all spoken language should be striving. This leads to the conclusion that *I cannot* is in some way better English than *I can't,* or that *It is I* is to be preferred to *It's me.* Linguistics, adopting as far as possible an objective approach, makes no value judgments of this kind, but simply notes that these different forms exist and that in certain circumstances one form may be more appropriate than another.

We have also seen that linguistics regards spoken language

as a worthy object of study. Because of its ephemeral nature, the spoken utterance is difficult to study, but modern recording techniques can help the linguist here. In the case of Western European languages it is sometimes difficult to make a distinction in grammar or in lexis between spoken and written language, but in some other languages, notably modern Greek, Arabic and Chinese, the distinction between the spoken and written language is very much greater. As such a distinction is so clear-cut in these languages, we may well wonder if there is no similar distinction in English, German, French and Spanish.

If we take a factual statement in English, and examine it closely, we may see what kind of distinction can be made between the spoken and the written language. In the sentence *The 'Daily Mail' has given an excellent account of the affair,* we have a sentence that might equally well occur in speech or in writing. If it occurs in writing it will take the form given above. If it occurs in speech, however, there are various forms it may take. We will leave aside the dozens of different regional pronunciations that might be given to this sentence and simply consider the possible stress variations that are common to them all. One might emphasise the words *'Daily Mail'*, to indicate that the account given by this paper is excellent, whereas that given by others is not. Or one might emphasize the word *excellent,* to imply praise for the *Daily Mail's* account, without necessarily making a comparison with other newspapers. Or one might emphasize the word *has* in order to deny a statement to the contrary. None of these variations is possible in the written language, unless we resort to italics or underlining, which in themselves are only an attempt to represent in writing some of the subtleties of speech. But there is more to it than this. Each of the words *has, an,* and *of* has two forms in speech, these are: /haz/ and /həz/, /an/ and /ən/, /ɔv/ and /əv/. An Englishman reading the sentence aloud is compelled to decide which form he is going to use. In certain circumstances he might consider that the first alternative in each case was more appropriate, but if using the sentence in rapid conversation, he would almost certainly say: /həz/,

/ ən / and / əv /. The speaker selects one of a number of possible interpretations, which are not distinguished in the written mode.

There is then a difference between spoken and written English. We could examine many other aspects of this difference. In lexicology, for example, many words are much more common in writing than they are in speech, and some that often occur in speech are rare in writing. In grammar too, there are differences. Anyone who has had to prepare for printing a typescript taken from a tape-recording of an extempore speech will be well aware of the great difference between the spoken language and the written language. What was perfectly acceptable in speech becomes impossible in a carefully prepared document.

These differences do not only apply to spoken and written English, but exist in other Western European languages as well. In fact in French and German the differences are probably greater than in English. In addition to differences of the kind that we have already noticed, there are in French certain forms that have no representation in speech. For example, *Les fleurs qu'elle m'a données* is a sentence in which the final *-es* of *données* is regarded as an essential part of the grammatical construction in writing. Yet it is not represented in speech at all. In German the distinction between various adjectival endings, such as *-en* or *-em,* is often very indistinctly made in speech, but in writing such distinctions are essential.

A further examination of this question reveals that the broad distinction between spoken and written language, in Western European languages at any rate, is complicated by variations within these two categories. This has been considered by Spencer and Gregory in *An Approach to the Study of Style.*[1] These authors use the term *mode of discourse* for the range of these variations, which they refer to as 'the dimension which accounts for the linguistic differences which result from the distinction between spoken and written discourse'. There is

[1] This monograph is contained in Enkvist, Spencer and Gregory, *Linguistics and Style,* O.U.P., 1964; see pp. 87 and 88.

a range here from the spontaneous spoken mode of everyday conversation unrelated to written language, to the most formal examples of the written mode, for example legal documents which are written without any intention on the part of the writer that they will necessarily be read aloud. In between these two extremes we have, within the written mode, language that is written to be read without concealing the fact that it is written language read aloud, for example a radio news bulletin; we have also written language that is intended to be spoken in such a way that it will give the illusion of spontaneous speech, for example dramatic dialogue. There are other distinctions of this kind within the written mode and a similar range within the spoken mode.

When languages are taught as a means of communication it is evident that to teach the language in its written mode is insufficient. A large part of communication is oral and for this purpose the spoken mode must be taught. Since there is a clear distinction between spoken and written language, and since some features of the spoken mode are not found in the written, we cannot teach written language alone and assume that pupils who have mastered this will be able to develop unassisted an ability to use the spoken language. For the pupils to produce acceptable spoken language an acceptable spoken language must be taught. This teaching of the spoken language cannot be based on a study of the written mode; such a procedure is a serious hindrance to satisfactory performance in using the spoken mode. A kind of 'schoolboy French' or 'schoolboy German' is often learned in this country, which is simply a spoken representation of the written language in the textbooks, and differs considerably from the spoken language normally used in France or Germany, especially in intonation, speed and the idiom of conversation. Persons who have learned only this unreal representation of the written mode are at a loss to understand or speak when confronted with the spoken mode as used by a native speaker, even in simple conversation. The assumption lying behind much of the language teaching and examining in Britain is that features of the written mode (for example, the use of the past tenses or the agreement of the past participle in written French, or the system of adjectival endings in written German) are vastly more important than features of the spoken languages, such as intonation patterns or the means by which emphasis is conveyed orally. If we could look at the whole matter as objectively as possible, and linguistics should help us to do this, there is no reason why features of one mode should not be given just as much importance as features of another.

In the great majority of cases what is required in Britain is teaching that gives instruction in both the spoken and the written modes, and in some of the principal variations within these modes. In this case, to neglect one mode at the expense of the other would be a serious deficiency in the teaching. Some learners, however, may need to use one mode more than another, and for some pupils the written mode may present too many difficulties; but in most cases both modes should be taught, and they will normally be taught concurrently. Modern techniques of audio-lingual teaching offer us the possibility of teaching the spoken language more thoroughly than ever before. It can now be taught without reference to the written language. It is not necessary to conduct oral exercises in the classroom on the basis of the printed page in front of the pupils. The recorded voice and the visual image on screen or flannelgraph can replace the written language of the textbook and the whole lesson can concentrate on the spoken mode. This does not mean that the written language would necessarily be neglected; it would be taught separately. The spoken language can be taught independently of it.

The teaching of spoken language presents some linguistic problems to the teacher, which he may be inadequately equipped to resolve, and with which linguistics can give him valuable help. For example, in teaching the forms of French adjectives that mark agreement with masculine or feminine nouns it is usually stated that an 'e' is added to the masculine form to obtain the feminine form (e.g. *vert, verte*). This is a rule of the written language. How can we describe the forms of French adjectives without reference to the written language? It may be possible to do this by saying that the final consonant sound of the feminine is dropped to obtain the masculine form, e.g.

verte	/vɛrt/	*vert*	/vɛr/
chaude	/ʃod/	*chaud*	/ʃo/
douce	/dus/	*doux*	/du/
longue	/lɔ̃g/	*long*	/lɔ̃/

A full linguistic study of this would need to be made in any detailed description of spoken French.[1] As a second example, we find that, as far as written French is concerned, the system of the demonstrative adjective and its use has been well described. The forms concerned are four in number: *ce, cet, cette, ces*. In the spoken language there are also four forms: /sə/, /sɛt/, /se/, /sez/. These do not correspond exactly with the four forms in the written mode, except in the case of the first. How can we describe briefly how each of these is used in the spoken language, without referring to the written mode? Here is a problem of linguistic description that the linguist should be able to resolve for the assistance of the teacher.

Structures

Traditional grammar has been very much concerned with accidence, that is, with the inflections of important words according to their function in the sentence. Highly inflected languages, such as Greek and Latin, have systems of accidence for various types of word that can be set out in paradigms. Thus the conjugations of Latin verbs and the declensions of Latin nouns have been set out in tabular form for pupils to study and learn. Traditional grammar then proceeds to the rules for the use of the various inflected forms; this involves the use of tenses, the agreement of verb and subject, of adjective and noun, and so on. While this type of grammar has been extensively used for Greek and Latin, it is also used for the teaching of modern languages, some of which are not nearly so highly inflected as the ancient languages. Grammars of

[1] For a fuller treatment of this question, see R. L. Politzer, *Teaching French: An Introduction to Applied Linguistics,* Ginn, 1960, pp. 79, 80.

modern languages often have this dual basis in accidence on the one hand, and the use of the forms that accidence provides on the other.

In the case of English and French, as well as some other modern languages, this approach to grammar is in danger of neglecting important aspects of the construction of sentences. In these modern languages the order in which words are arranged and the way in which they are fitted together in groups and clauses, are just as important as the inflections of words according to their function. The construction of sentences follows certain regular patterns and the nature of these patterns can be considered the basis of grammar. A type of linguistic study has developed, very largely in America under the influence of Bloomfield and others, that considers the *structure* of the sentence, as we are describing it, to be vital to any adequate grammar. This structuralist approach does not neglect accidence, but regards it as one element in the structure of the sentence.

The structuralist view of language has led to the development in language teaching of an activity known as *pattern practice*.[1] This is a type of exercise, usually conducted orally, that sets out to give practice in the use of certain structures or patterns. Pattern practice does not involve translation, and does not involve constructing sentences deductively by the application of abstract rules. It is a type of exercise which is often intentionally simple. A certain structure is repeated frequently by the pupil in various ways using varying vocabulary. Normally, an example sentence is given by the teacher, and the pupil is then asked to change a certain part of the sentence in response to stimuli given by the teacher. For example:

Teacher: *Je n'ai pas donné le livre à Marie.*
Pupil: *Je n'ai pas donné le livre à Marie.*
Teacher: *Le cahier.*
Pupil: *Je n'ai pas donné le cahier à Marie.*

[1] A more detailed explanation of pattern practice is given in R. Lado, *Language Teaching: A Scientific Approach*, McGraw-Hill, 1964, Chapter 11.

45

Teacher: *A Paul.*
Pupil: *Je n'ai pas donné le cahier à Paul.*
Teacher: *Il.*
Pupil: *Il n'a pas donné le cahier à Paul.*
Teacher: *Rendu.*
Pupil: *Il n'a pas rendu le cahier à Paul.*
Teacher: *Au professeur.*
Pupil: *Il n'a pas rendu le cahier au professeur.*

The words of the sentence have changed, but the structure remains. The pupil is being drilled in the use of this structure, which involves the compound tense, the positioning of the negative particles and the order of direct and indirect object.

Drills of this kind can also take the form of answers to questions. In this example in German the pupils are instructed to answer always in the affirmative using *Ja* and a complete sentence:

Teacher: *Hast du einen Brief geschrieben?*
Pupil: *Ja, ich habe einen Brief geschrieben.*
Teacher: *Hast du den roten Wagen gesehen?*
Pupil: *Ja, ich habe den roten Wagen gesehen.*
Teacher: *Hast du die Platten gespielt?*
Pupil: *Ja, ich habe die Platten gespielt.*

While drilling this structure of a sentence in the perfect tense, the use of the inflected forms of the definite and indefinite articles also enters into the exercise. Inflection is seen in this way to be part of the structure of the sentence.

Linguistics has greatly influenced the development of pattern practice, which now has an important place in language teaching, and which can be extensively used in language laboratories. As a teaching device pattern practice has serious dangers. Pupils may be taught to chant the patterns in exercises, but may still be unable to use them productively in speech. The extensive use of pattern practice in the classroom might become mere verbalising in which the pupil is learning parrot-fashion without any real grasp of meaning. In the next section of this chapter we shall consider contextualisation. and this should be regarded as complementary to the structuralist view of language teaching. Not only must we teach the structures of the language, but also how to use those structures meaningfully in a context. We must also note that there is something unreal about the German exercise quoted above. In real-life conversation the answers would probably not be in full sentences. An element of unreality inevitably creeps into language learning activities, but linguistics, in making a study of spoken language as it is, can help to prevent teaching from straying too far into unreality.

Teachers who wish to teach structures need a grammar of the language that sets out what the structures are. They also need information about which structures occur most frequently and about the grading of those structures for teaching. In starting to teach a language, a teacher can usually organise his linguistic material on a structural basis in the early stages. In starting French he may teach the structure: *Voici* + article and noun. He may recognise that this structure can be varied by using *Voilà* or *C'est* in the initial position. He may then go on to the structure: Article and noun + *être* + adverbial group; for example: *Le livre est sur la table.* He may then wish to introduce the structure: *Où* + *est* + article and noun. He may also bring in *Qu'est-ce qu c'est?* With these structures quite a lot of oral work is possible in the classroom. The teacher may then proceed to the structure: *Je suis* (or *Vous êtes* or *Êtes-vous*) + article + noun. By this time he is wondering if he has got his classification of structures right. *Vous êtes* and *Êtes-vous* seem to be quite different structures, and yet it is convenient to teach them together as different forms of the same structure. The teacher is now needing the help of linguistics to classify and grade the structures he is teaching. In any case, within a few weeks he will have progressed so far that he may have lost track of the structures he has taught and those he still has to teach. The presentation of basic sentence patterns by Paul Roberts in his book *English Sentences*,[1] is the kind of work that should greatly assist language teachers in organising their linguistic material for the systematic teaching of structures. The linguistic theory of *transformation*, clearly explained by

[1] P. Roberts, *English Sentences*, Harcourt, Brace, 1962.

Roberts in his book, can be a great help in the construction of suitable exercises. The theory, which derives from Chomsky,[1] postulates that there is a fairly small set of sentence patterns—the basic sentence patterns—and that all other sentences are *transformations* of these, that is, they are variations on a basic pattern. The basic pattern shown in *A man is here* is transformed in the sentence *There is a man here*. The passive construction is a transformation of the active construction, so that *John loves Mary* can be transformed into *Mary is loved by John*.

Such transformations can clearly form the basis for pattern practice in which pupils would simply be asked to make transformations of basic patterns according to certain rules for generating fresh sentences. The teacher who is designing programmes for use in a language laboratory needs the help of the linguist here. The linguist can set out the basic patterns and the transformations. Equipped with this information about the structure of the language the teacher can then construct the programmes that he needs for a particular class according to the knowledge of vocabulary and grammar that that class may already have. Many teachers who use language laboratories have, understandably enough, found it essential to devise their own programmes. This task could be made much simpler if they were aware of the work of the linguists in analysing the structure of the language, and if the results of linguists' work could be made readily available to teachers.

Context of Situation

A further significant contribution of linguistics to language teaching has been the elucidation of what linguists sometimes call *contextualization*. This is the relationship of the actual substance and form of a piece of language to the situation in which it is used. It is this relationship that gives to language what we call meaning. Taking the English sentence *What's*

[1] Noam Chomsky, of the Massachusetts Institute of Technology, is the linguist primarily responsible for expounding the transformation theory. His book, *Syntactic Structures*, The Hague, 1957, is too difficult to be attempted by any reader who has not done considerable work in linguistics. An admirable introduction to the theory is Roberts, *op. cit.*

that? we must admit that these words, as cold black print on the page, have no vital significance. If we wish to describe their meaning we have to clothe them with a context, we have to place them in a situation. While I am calmly talking to my neighbour over the garden fence, there is suddenly a loud explosion in the street nearby. My neighbour starts with alarm and exclaims, *What's that?* The words now have significance. The British linguist, J. R. Firth, wrote: 'Meaning is best regarded . . . as a complex of relations of various kinds between the component terms of a context of situation'.[1] If we think of the sentence, *Who are you?* we cannot imagine its meaning without thinking of the elements of a situation in which someone is questioned by someone else. To abstract the meaning from such a situation is impossible, and the 'complex of relations' begins to develop as we add bewildered surprise, puzzled curiosity or simple ignorance to the motives of the speaker.

For convenience we are often obliged to label vocabulary items with a meaning in another language. We have to provide equivalents in the mother-tongue. But often we know that these are approximations rather than equivalents. Only a 'complex of relations of various kinds between the component terms of a context of situation' can really give the meaning of a word. Even words so simple as *la maison* and *la route* do not convey to a French mind exactly what *the house* and *the road* do to an Englishman. Any method of teaching which gives pupils the notion that word-for-word equivalents in one language can convey the meaning of sentences in another, is failing to teach an understanding of language in its widest sense.[2]

For this reason great advantage attaches to audio-visual courses, which can place any utterance in a situation suggested

[1] J. R. Firth, *The Tongues of Men,* and *Speech,* reprinted by O.U.P., 1964, p. 110. Firth, who was Professor of General Linguistics in the University of London from 1942 to 1956, exerted a very strong influence over a group of British linguists whose work has developed considerably since Firth's death.

[2] For a linguistic treatment of translation and the question of equivalents in different languages, see J. C. Catford, *A Linguistic Theory of Translation,* O.U.P., 1965.

by the visual element. This does not mean that the picture will necessarily define the meaning of the utterance, but the context of the utterance is set out in the visual representation of a situation, so that the meaning, defined maybe by other means, is rendered more accurate in association with the context. It would be idle to suggest that linguists invented audio-visual language teaching. In fact Comenius[1] thought of it and practised it, long before the linguists of today propounded their views. But what has happened is that a linguistic theory of the 'context of situation' has influenced language teaching by confirming audio-visual methods that teachers themselves were developing.

Tasks for Linguists

These are but some of the ways in which linguistics has assisted language teaching today and may continue to do so in the future. The work of French linguists at Saint-Cloud, which resulted in the production of *Le Français Fondamental,* is often quoted as an example of the practical help that linguists can give to language teachers. The account of this work has been given elsewhere,[2] and it has also been criticised. Linguists can be expected to improve their methods and the effectiveness of their work, so that in work that is now being undertaken we can hope that there will be even more valuable assistance for language teaching.

Professor Strevens has very clearly set out the research needs of language teaching,[3] and among these needs are many which lie in the field of linguistics. The development of descriptions of languages, that set out fully all the features of the languages being described, is clearly the task of the academic linguists.

[1] Comenius (1592-1670), the Moravian pedagogue, developed in his *Orbis sensualium pictus,* 1658, a system for teaching Latin by means of pictures.

[2] M. A. K. Halliday, A. McIntosh and P. Strevens, *The Linguistic Sciences and Language Teaching,* Longmans, 1964, pp. 190-8. This is a readily accessible and concise account. Fuller information is given in Gougenheim et al., *L'Elaboration du Français Elémentaire,* Paris, 1956.

[3] See P. D. Strevens, 'Linguistic Research and Language Teaching', in *New Trends in Linguistic Research,* Council for Cooperation of the Council of Europe, 1963. This article also appears in P. D. Strevens, *Papers in Language and Language Teaching,* O.U.P., 1965.

More limited descriptions of certain aspects of a language for teaching purposes are also needed. The work at Saint-Cloud was an example of this, but other projects have been and are being undertaken for other languages. An analysis of the German language by Pfeffer is to be published over the next few years. At the Language Centre of the University of Essex a scheme has been undertaken for a large-scale analysis of present day spoken and written Russian. It is intended in this scheme not only to carry out the task of vocabulary selection for teaching purposes, but to extend the analysis to grammar and phonology. Such a project will produce the linguistic data needed for the production of various types of courses. In the case of Afro-Asian languages contrastive analyses are needed to provide a basis for teaching such languages to Europeans. Specialized studies of some aspects of familiar languages are also required. The Nuffield Foreign Languages Teaching Materials Project[1] found that not nearly enough was known about the language of primary school children in England and France, and it has been necessary for the Project to initiate research into children's use of language to assist in the production of an adequate language course for teaching.

No attempt has been made in this chapter to give a full account of linguistics; books on general linguistics, of which a number are available, can provide the reader with this.[2] All we have sought to do here is to indicate the relevance of linguistics for language teaching by giving a few practical examples. We shall see, in later chapters, how the work in linguistics which we have mentioned lies at the basis of most of the new developments now taking place in language teaching. Tape-recorders, language laboratories, cine-loops, films and television are all of very little value to the language teacher unless the linguistic material to be presented is adequately organised. It may well be that the academic science of linguistics, and its applied branches, will ultimately prove to be the most powerful factor in improving our language teaching.

[1] More information about the Nuffield Project is given on pp. 162-164.

[2] e.g. R. H. Robins, *General Linguistics: An Introductory Survey*, Longmans, 1964. This book itself also contains an excellent general bibliography and more detailed bibliographies for each chapter.

4

Towards a Theory of Language Teaching

Linguistics is concerned with language and how it operates. It provides us with a very large part of the theoretical basis of language teaching. But there is also a theoretical basis for language teaching in the study of the psychological processes involved. The teacher of languages is concerned not only with the nature of language, but also with the nature of the mental processes by which the use of language is learned. Any fresh development in language teaching is dependent to a large extent on theoretical ideas of language on the one hand and of the language learning process on the other. To complete our consideration of the background to current developments, we need now to look at some theories of language teaching and to note what are the ideas, drawn largely from the field of psychology, that underlie much that is now taking place. The present state of our knowledge is unable to give us unequivocal answers to some of the most urgent questions about language learning. All we can do here is to consider these questions and notice what are the significant conceptions that emerge.

Direct Method Theory

We have already seen what were the leading ideas of the Direct Methodists at the end of the nineteenth century. Their writings are rather too polemical to provide us with a coherent theory of language learning, but certain assumptions either lie behind their work or, more usually, are explicitly stated by them. First, they believed that language should be taught initially through speech, that the spoken language should take precedence over written language in order of presentation to the pupil. Viëtor, Gouin and Francke all say this, and Thirion, a French teacher in England, wrote in 1888: 'French is a living tongue, yet English people resolve it shall be taught as if a dead one. . . . Grammar should not be the starting point. The four aims of language teaching in their proper order are: Hearing, Speaking, Reading, Writing.'[1]

Secondly, they were opposed to translation as a teaching instrument, because it involved a mental exercise that was far removed from the normal experience of spontaneous speech. They thought that language was to be learned by using language rather than by laboriously constructing sentences, piecing together the necessary words according to the grammatical rules. In attacking this process they went so far as to say that the real unit of language was the sentence rather than the word. While it was useful to say this at that time, the statement is in fact extreme; words do have a significant existence as language units, and even illiterate language speakers are conscious of this. In reacting against the translation method of their day the Direct Methodists were certainly right, though it must not be assumed that translation has no part to play in language learning. Some very successful systems, such as the Bilingual Method used in Wales,[2] are really based on translation. Nevertheless the preference for oral work, based on a reader or on passages for reading, was in itself fundamentally sound and showed a clearer insight into the language learning process than did the ideas of those who favoured grammar and translation.

A third, and most vital idea of the Direct Methodists was that of direct association between the new word in the language being learned and the object, action or idea designated by that word. There was to be no intervention of the mother tongue. This direct association really means a link in

[1] Quoted by M. Gilbert in 'The Origins of the Reform Movement in Modern Language Teaching in England', in the *Durham Research Review*, Vol. I, No. 4, Sept. 1953, p. 8.

[2] See C. J. Dodson, *The Bilingual Method*, Aberystwyth: Faculty of Education, University College of Wales, 1962.

the mind between the new word and the concept of the object designated. It presupposes that concepts exist independently of language in the mind. But this is by no means proved; indeed it often seems that the nature of many mental concepts is dictated by the words and structures of the language normally used by the individual. H. E. Palmer, as we have seen, criticised this point in the theory of the Direct Method, and claimed that the most 'direct' way of conveying the meaning of a new word might often be simply to give a translation into the learner's native language. Other supposedly 'direct' methods of supplying meaning, e.g. explanation or definition in the target language, were often hopelessly cumbersome and sometimes quite ineffective.[1]

There were two other important ideas of the Direct Methodists. One of these was the importance they attached to phonetics, which stemmed from their firm belief in the priority of speech and from the fact that many of them were phoneticians. While phonetics in its broadest sense must inevitably enter into any oral language teaching, it was probably a mistake to formalise this as much as men such as Paul Passy tried to do. A rigorous use of phonetic script does not necessarily secure a good pronunciation, and it can confuse and complicate the work of the learner unnecessarily. Finally, the inductive teaching of grammar was advocated. This again may have been more a reaction against bad methods of teaching than a theory formulated for its own sake. Those who have seriously tried to teach grammar inductively will know how long it takes and how uncertain it can be. Yet it is certainly possible to learn a language, and learn it well, without learning the formal rules of grammar. However, a certain amount of work on grammatical rules does in fact speed and simplify the language learning process.

The Direct Methodists had some excellent ideas; in fact they were right most of the time. But their ideas were rather extreme and needed modifying in practice. This modification is what the exponents of the Compromise or Oral Method

[1] H. E. Palmer, *The Scientific Study and Teaching of Languages*, Harrap, 1917, pp. 77-103.

attempted to undertake. The difficulty is that the result remained something of a compromise, without a clearly defined theory of its own. Belyayev describes this situation by saying: 'The most rational and only correct method of teaching must obviously be one which differs from the translation–grammatical method by throwing more weight on the side of linguistic practice, and from the direct method by encouraging the theoretical understanding of this practice.'[1] But the question is: how much practice and how much understanding? Fries recommended 85 per cent of class time for practice and 15 per cent for explanation and commentary.[2] The fact remains that we are still seeking a fully comprehensive theory of language teaching that will account for what takes place in language learning and guide us in our procedures of method.

An 'Oral Method' Theory

While there has been this measure of uncertainty about the basic nature of language learning, and while a scientifically based theory has not been available, a certain theory of language teaching has grown up in our schools which has received wide acceptance. This theory may not have been clearly formulated in any published work, nor given a title of its own, but it exists in the minds of many teachers throughout the country. It flourishes under the general umbrella of the so-called Oral Method, and it can justify its existence because it achieves the desired result. Pupils taught by those who hold this theory get passes at Ordinary and Advanced levels; they may in time become very proficient users of a foreign language.

A statement of this theory, as it might be expounded during break in the staff-room, would run something like this: 'Of course, you have to give them as much oral work as possible, especially in the early years, when they take to it quite well. But there is a lot of vocabulary to be learned and grammatical

[1] B. V. Belyayev, *The Psychology of Teaching Foreign Languages*, Pergamon Press, 1963, p. 218. Belyayev is Professor of Methodology in the University of Moscow. His book was published by the Ministry of Education of the R.S.F.S.R. in 1959, and has been translated into English by R. F. Hingley.

[2] Quoted by R. Lado in *Language Teaching: A Scientific Approach*, McGraw-Hill, 1964, p. 55.

work to be covered for G.C.E., and there is not time for very much oral work on only four periods a week. In any case, we teach them the basic elements of the language in vocabulary and grammar, and if they get hold of this work they have then got a foundation that they can build on later. When they come to go abroad, if they ever do, they may be tongue-tied for the first week or two, but the work they have done here stands them in good stead, and they will be able to develop fluency gradually; whereas if they had not done any French at all at school they would be completely lost.'

It must be said that in the main this theory works. Pupils so taught do in fact remember the basic grammar when they go abroad and, if they stay there long enough, develop a considerable capacity to speak the language. The theory leaves great opportunity for the enterprising teacher to develop conversational work, use B.B.C. language broadcasts, indulge in dramatic work or conduct school parties abroad. Some of the language teaching that has been done in this way has been very successful.

The majority of schools today are teaching languages in the climate of compromise which this theory, as expounded by our imaginary schoolmaster, can scarcely conceal. Even where audio-visual courses and language laboratories are in use there is often an uneasy alliance of the methods and principles these imply and the old routine of grammar and translation. It is hardly surprising then to find that this theory of language learning leaves us with all sorts of inconsistencies and contradictions. If our practice in the early years is based on the belief that language is to be learned by using the language orally, why do we deviate from this so frequently in the fourth and fifth years of the secondary school course? It is hard to believe that the demands of the traditional Ordinary level provide the sole reason for this. Indeed the difficulty teachers are finding in developing courses that will suitably follow an audio-visual course used in the first two years, and that will lead on to the new types of Ordinary level, suggests that we do not really know how to teach by predominantly oral methods throughout the school. Secondly, while it is possible to develop fluency at a later stage, say five to ten years after leaving school, must we inevitably accept that for most pupils a fluent command of the spoken language cannot be obtained in five years at school? If pupils begin to talk freely in French, within a strictly limited range, during their first year, as they often do, why cannot this be steadily developed to a reasonable conversational facility in most everyday situations by the time the pupils are in their fifth year? Thirdly, we may have serious doubts about a study of the grammar of the written language providing a basis for a command of the spoken language later on. This seems to be a denial of the order of priorities to which many teachers at least pay lip-service: hearing, speaking, reading, writing.

These are some of the uncertainties that have beset modern language teaching for many years. It may be that we are still not much nearer a solution of these questions. But at this point it is useful to review what we know about the way a child learns his L1, and about the differences between this and the learning of an L2. Even if we cannot formulate a full theory of language learning, some helpful ideas will be found.

Learning the Mother Tongue

Our understanding of the psychological processes by which an infant learns to use language is far from complete. We must in the main limit ourselves to the observable behaviour of the child without making too many conjectures about what is taking place in his mind. We must remember too that the infant is learning in all spheres of activity; his mental and physical powers are developing and he is gradually exploring his environment and what it offers, while at the same time he is learning to understand and to use speech. He is learning to eat, to crawl, to play and to speak all at the same time. In all these activities he learns largely by trial and error and by conditioned responses. But normally he is assisted in a number of ways. First, the speech that he hears—mainly the speech of his parents, brothers and sisters or other members of the family—is naturally limited in range. As he spends most of his time in the relative security of his home and in his mother's company, he is not thrust into the complications of advanced technical vocabularies or unusual styles. It is a simple everyday vocabulary that he usually hears. This is true in almost all circumstances in which children are brought up. Furthermore, he has relatively long periods of exposure to the language. Circumstances may vary, but the infant who is learning to speak usually spends several hours each day listening to speech or attempting speech himself. The affectionate attention of his parents and others also helps him. He is spoken to lovingly and encouraged to respond orally. Where this parental affection is lacking speech development is often retarded.

After the first two or three months of his life, during which his cries are determined solely by his physical needs, the infant passes through a stage of *babbling,* when he appears to be experimenting with his vocal organs. He makes a wide range of baby noises, and sometimes seems to be listening to his own efforts or discovering the possibilities of his own organs of speech. All the while he has opportunities to listen to speech from others, though comprehension comes only very gradually. By about eleven months of age he can usually discriminate certain basic patterns of speech and will respond to certain commands from his parents or others. The age at which a child begins to speak varies widely, but at about the age of twelve months, or soon after, he begins to make deliberate sounds which have significance for him and others. These are often monosyllables or duplicated syllables, such as *mum-mum, bye-bye,* or the French *dodo,* which are partly a genuine baby language, employing different morphemes from those of the adult language, and partly a training in phonetics by repetition. It is easier to say the same syllable twice, or two very similar syllables, than to say two that are completely different. Even when he can make himself understood by two or three word sentences such as *Daddy gone,* he may still be unable to distinguish certain phonemes and may pronounce *car, cat, tea, teddy* all with initial /t/. But all the time he is highly motivated to improve his performance in the language; he has wants that require expression and he has a constant desire, probably not consciously formulated, to understand more and to say more. His learning is reinforced by success when he finds that his utterances are understood. This is hardly a conscious process, yet it must be a realisation that his speech is effective and acceptable that makes the child gradually conform to the norm.

In the early years parents and others usually give the child a good deal of encouragement to speak. They may adopt a form of baby language themselves, which is in effect a way of simplifying language for the child. They may repeat a simple phrase or sentence far more frequently in playing with the child than they would in adult conversation. Later on there comes a stage when most parents correct the child in matters of speech. This may be an effort to eradicate false analogies in the child's speech, such as *buyed* or *fighted,* or it may be the effort to teach the child a desired variety of pronunciation and speech rather than the variety acquired from contact with playmates.

There comes a stage of development which has been called the *naming stage,* when the child's vocabulary begins to expand rapidly. Usually before the compulsory school age the child has enough command of the language to ask constant questions, such as *What's that?* or *What's that called?* which all tend to equip him with more words. These constant enquiries are not of course purely linguistic, and are as much an expression of the desire to find out about things and situations around as an effort to learn more words. By the time the child starts school he is equipped with a surprisingly large vocabulary. J. B. Carroll estimates that the first grade pupil in an American school may know as many as 7,500 morphemes.[1]

All this learning takes place without reference to the written language. Some children learn to read in the pre-school years, it is true, but these are the rare exceptions. Many adults find it difficult to learn new words, or to learn a new language, without seeing the words in writing. But all of us once learned our mother tongue without thinking of the possibility of committing speech to writing, indeed we probably had no real

[1] J. B. Carroll, *Language and Thought,* Englewood Cliffs, New Jersey: Prentice Hall, 1964, p. 32.

understanding of what writing was. We should not forget that it is possible, in childhood at least, to learn to speak a language without any acquaintance with the written mode of discourse.

Second Language Learning

Gouin and other Direct Methodists advocated that the learning of a second language should be made to resemble more closely the learning of the mother tongue by a child. In many respects this was a very sound principle, but there are fundamental differences between the two processes.

Whereas the child spends a large part of each day in some language activity—listening to others or making attempts to speak himself—the adult learning a second language may have only a few hours per week to devote to this. There may be compensation for this in the concentrated nature of adult learning and in systematic teaching. But the great amount of time available to the child makes a fundamental difference. Partly on account of this, some have been led to think that language learning should ideally be a full-time activity for a certain period. The ASTP courses in America during the war were full-time courses lasting nine months, and they achieved remarkable results. Such a course gives the learner the opportunity to be quite immersed in the foreign language, to absorb its structures into his way of thinking and speaking, so that he develops some feeling for the language. Crash courses for businessmen in this country of recent years have taken a similar form. But in school work such a course is hardly a possibility.

The adolescent or the adult struggling to learn a foreign tongue often has far less motivation than the child. An infant is really obliged to learn to speak, he wants to do so, and indeed he could not live normally unless he did. These factors very rarely operate with the same force in the case of the L2 learner. Often the foreign language is simply a subject on the school timetable which one may or may not like; there are not the same compelling reasons for learning. Where a person is suddenly thrown down in a foreign language community or is obliged to learn a language to accomplish some vital task, there is usually much greater success than in the more academic situation of normal school work. Connected also with this question of motivation is the whole matter of the mental development of the individual. In the case of the child, the learning of the mother tongue is one aspect of normal mental development, in which language assists thought. The adult learner is a person whose mind is already formed to a very large extent, and who is capable of making rational abstractions or generalisations about any learning activity. The infant cannot do this and therefore learns at a level below conscious thought and concentration. To try to make the adult learn in exactly the same way would be to waste the adult's powers of abstract thought and his ability to generalise. Yet these adult powers must be used to arrive at the same end as that which the child achieves—mastery of the basic language skills.

As we have seen, the language a child is learning is almost automatically limited for the child by the circumstances in which he lives. For the adult learner this limitation has to be carefully organised. There is no point in starting the beginner on a difficult literary or technical text. The language must be presented in manageable units and with a systematic grading from the simple to the more difficult. The child uses the language he is learning for the affectionate and intimate experiences of life. He speaks to his mother and his mother speaks to him. Her voice, using the language he is learning, will have a soothing, reassuring or affectionate tone for him. He will use the language to express joy, pain, terror, expectation, love. Many words will thus take on for him particular emotional overtones which probably tend to endear the language itself to him. The adult or adolescent learner of a foreign language usually meets that language in an atmosphere in which the words on the page of the course book are not charged with any real emotional significance, but are on the contrary associated with the classroom, with homework, with examinations and so on. We shall see that the project of teaching a foreign language to younger children, and the situational approach in audio-visual courses, involve an attempt to relate language to the real situations of life which often clothe language with affective overtones.

The adult learner, as we have already noticed may wish to write down new words or to see them printed. He has often been so conditioned to the printed page that he finds it difficult to retain a purely aural impression of a word or phrase in a foreign language. This certainly constitutes a difference between infant learning and adult learning; it may be in addition a real disadvantage to the adult learner who wishes to master a spoken foreign language. Adult learners may be more seriously inhibited in oral work because of a shyness in making unfamiliar speech sounds in the hearing of others. Speech is something about which adults are far more sensitive than small children. The adult may also expect too much from himself and soon experience frustration and disappointment. Language learning is a more difficult undertaking than many people suppose and in any case needs much time, patience and perseverance. But the greatest difficulty of all for the adult learner is that he has acquired one language already. His mind can never be a *tabula rasa*. The concepts of the first language are firmly fixed in the mind and the new language is learned in relation to these. The new language is, so to speak, grafted on to the concepts of the first language. The English learner meets the French word *la rue* and learns that this means *the street,* but *la rue* is often used when one would say *the road* in English, so that the concepts underlying these words in the two languages do not correspond, and a new set of concepts has to be formed in the mind as well as a new set of words. This *interference* of concepts of the L1 not only affects the understanding of meaning, but can also produce incorrect structures, as we saw in our previous chapter. It constitutes one of the major problems of L2 learning.

Few would now advocate that in teaching an L2 we should try to recapture the conditions in which the L1 was learned. This is in fact impossible. In teaching adolescents or adults it is a mistake to fail to use their mental powers to full advantage. But we have seen from this brief survey of L1 and L2 learning that there is some point in the limitation of linguistic items, that language needs to be related to emotional experiences, that it is possible to learn aurally without recourse to writing, and that the dangers of interference need to be overcome.

Knowledge, Skills and Habits

Learning a language is a different educational exercise from learning most other school subjects. It is not primarily a matter of acquiring certain knowledge, of absorbing certain facts, nor is it a development of such knowledge in academic thought processes or attitudes. It is true that there is far more to geography, history, physics or biology than simply absorbing facts in the mind, but facts observed or recorded are the essential raw material of these subjects. They are basically descriptive subjects which proceed from description to develop ideas. The use of language, on the other hand, is a skill. If it were concerned mainly with facts, then it would be possible to teach certain vocabulary lists and teach a certain body of grammatical rules, and on the strength of this, claim to have taught the language. What would be lacking would be the essential elements of linguistic activity—aural perception of speech, comprehension of oral signals, manipulation of sentence structure, articulation, fluency, and so on. In this respect teaching a language is more like teaching a person to play a violin or to drive a car. You can explain to anybody how to drive a car in ten minutes or less, but it may take weeks to teach him to master the skills involved.

Belyayev has considerably elucidated this question of language teaching. He starts by distinguishing *language*, which he calls 'a means of communication', from *speech*, which is for him 'the process of communication carried out by means of language'.[1] It is possible to study a language without acquiring the ability to use that language in speech. This means that in consciously studying a language a person acquires certain theoretical knowledge about that language, it may be of its grammar, or of its vocabulary, or even of its phonology. But if he is to use that language in speech he must develop the appropriate speech *habits* and *skills*. Language teaching has

[1] Belyayev, *op. cit.*, p. 69.

these two closely linked, but not identical aspects: (*a*) pupils are made to study the language, and (*b*) they are taught to master speech in the language.

The definition given by Belyayev of habits and skills is very important for understanding the relationship between these two, and between them and knowledge. He says:

'Skill is the term given to an action accomplished by a person for the first time and with understanding. But this is a very different thing from speech habits, because by habit is understood an action carried out by a person without participation of consciousness, i.e. automatically owing to the fact that he has frequently carried out this action in the past.' [1]

From this definition Belyayev concludes that a habit is developed by the frequent repetition of a skill, and it cannot be developed simply by applying knowledge. To teach by progressing from knowledge to habits is inconsistent with psychology, because the exercise of skills, those actions that are performed with the participation of consciousness, is necessary for developing habits.

In the study and use of language, knowledge is clearly the perception and understanding of facts about the language, for example the rules of grammar, the declensions of nouns, and so on. Habits are those actions performed in using language which need no conscious thought—the pronunciation of particular sounds and words, even the choice of words in many cases, or the use of certain intonation patterns. The speaker does not consciously think of these things while he speaks. Skills, in Belyayev's sense, are those actions in speech which are consciously thought out—the conscious choice of an effective word, the moulding of a sentence, the intentional placing of emphasis, and so on. Frequently we form a sentence that we may never have used or heard before in exactly the same form. It is a new act of speech consciously performed. This Belyayev calls a skill.

He then points out two erroneous views of language teaching. First, to ask a pupil to construct his speech simply on the

[1] Belyayev, *op cit.*, p. 76.

basis of 'remembered grammatical rules',[1] expecting him to put theoretical knowledge immediately into practice, is to make the mistake of proceeding from knowledge to habits and to disregard the importance of skills. Second, teaching which makes repetition the basis of language learning, which requires endless repetition of correct phrases and sentences, is developing habits, but not giving adequate opportunity for the development of skills. The first of these views errs on the side of knowledge, the other on the side of habits, whereas for Belyayev the most important objective in the language lesson should be the development of skills. Knowledge and habits form a necessary basis for speech activity, but the essence of speech lies in the creative function of skills. 'When using language, a person always creates his speech anew, making creative use both of habits and knowledge.'[2]

Belyayev sees three activities in language teaching. First, knowledge about the language must be taught; second, habits must be developed by the frequent performance of single actions; and third, and most important, pupils must be exercised in the use of the skills involved in speaking, reading and writing.

This theory has much to commend it and appears to strike a fair balance between the grammar–translation method and the Direct Method; it is a useful basis too for many present-day developments in language teaching. But we may find some of Belyayev's statements too dogmatic, and his distinction between skills and habits may be rather too rigid to be real. It must also be realised that he speaks of a skill as an action, whereas we more normally think of a skill as the ability to perform an action; this may make his theory a little confusing to English readers. It is interesting that the American linguist Lado uses the term *facility* to cover, broadly speaking, what Belyayev would call *skills* and *habits*. Lado defines a facility as 'ease in using a language unit or pattern'. He continues:

'Learning a second language then involves acquiring varying degrees of facility for each phoneme and sequence of

[1] Belyayev, *op. cit.*, p. 76.
[2] Belyayev, *op. cit.*, p. 77.

phonemes; for each word, part of word, and pattern of words; for the parts of speech, modification structures, and parts of sentences; and for each sentence type and sequence of sentences. These facilities must be learned so that they can operate when attention is on the content and the thread of the argument and not on the expression items.'[1]

Both these writers then agree that language teaching is a matter of developing certain abilities in the pupils, whether we call these skills, habits or facilities, and these abilities must be so well learned that they can when necessary function without the aid of conscious effort.

A Suggested Synthesis

We can perhaps now pick out the leading ideas about language teaching that we have considered in this chapter and in the preceding one. It is to be hoped that at some time ideas such as these, drawn from the related fields of linguistics, psychology and practical pedagogy, will be constructed into one coherent theory of language teaching. At the moment there is not adequate knowledge about the language learning process, nor enough agreement among linguists and teachers, to build up such a theory in a way that would be generally acceptable. It is however possible to discern that certain ideas have been at the basis of the new developments in language teaching which are described in this book. None of these ideas is strikingly new, though some may be framed now in a new form. Some have been important in language teaching for many years, or have gradually gained increased acceptance over a long period. The list given here is not exhaustive; other points could be added. Not all of these points are of equal importance, and different teachers would attach far more importance to some than to others. But here are the principal ideas about language teaching that seem to underlie current developments in schools and colleges:

1 To learn a language is *to acquire new behaviour patterns*. This means that there are fresh *skills* and *habits* to be learned,

[1] Lado, *op. cit.*, p. 39.

and these can only be learned by constant practice, which is therefore central to language learning.

2 *The use of the spoken language* is essential to any language learning. Only by using the spoken language can there be adequate practice in the skills involved. The natural order in which language activities should be taught is (i) aural comprehension, (ii) oral expression, (iii) reading comprehension, (iv) expression in writing.

3 The linguistic items to be presented to the learner need careful *limitation* and *grading*.

4 The learner must master the *structures* of the language. This is even more vital than an extensive knowledge of vocabulary, because without structure, especially sentence structure, language cannot operate at all.

5 Linguistic items presented to the learner must be placed in a *context*. It is the situation in which an item of language is used that makes its meaning clear and provides affective overtones.

6 Useful *comparisons with the mother tongue* can greatly assist language learning. This does not mean translation, but an emphasis on those aspects of the target language in which the interference of the mother tongue could spoil the learner's achievement. Such work must be based on a contrastive analysis of the two languages.

With these ideas in mind we shall turn in Part Two to consider what is now taking place in language teaching and examining in Britain. We shall see to what extent these ideas are implied in the newer techniques. Sometimes two or more of these ideas come into conflict, as, for example, when the drilling of structures comes into opposition with the idea of situation. There are teachers who would not readily accept all these ideas. Some would not admit the primacy of the spoken language, others would not see language learning as the acquiring of new behaviour patterns, but rather as a discipline for the mind or as a cultural activity. But these ideas have sufficient in common to hang together and to be part of one unified movement in language teaching. In fact it is because these ideas come up at all levels of education from the primary school to the university that we can discern unifying elements in developments now taking place. If there is a new pattern in our language teaching at all, it is because the same unifying ideas have infused themselves throughout our educational system.

Part Two

Current Developments

5

New Techniques

In recent years technology has provided education with a range of teaching aids that have been a great help to modern language teaching. Foremost among these aids is the tape-recorder, which provides immediate facilities for recording the speech of either student or teacher and for replaying this speech as soon, and as often, as may be required. There are other advantages, such as ease of operation, which make the tape-recorder superior to the record-player for many purposes. The tape-recorder is the essential item of equipment that has made possible the development of audio-visual and audio-lingual courses, and which is basic to the language laboratory. Improved means of visual projection have at the same time facilitated the development of various types of visual aid which have been used in language courses. Radio and television, especially the latter, are playing a most important part in language teaching in different parts of the world, not only in schools, but also to the general public in their homes and elsewhere. Television offers special opportunities for audio-visual teaching. Linked with the growing use of these technological aids has been the development of programmed learning, which is also making its impact on language teaching.

We are now going to review the current developments in language teaching that have exploited these new teaching aids. All these developments have taken place against the background which we have surveyed in Part One. In this chapter we shall consider various new teaching techniques, new types of courses and new methods of teaching, while in the following one we shall examine the special opportunities and problems of language laboratories.

Audio-visual Courses

Let us consider first of all what are often called audio-visual courses. These are courses which present the language by means of some kind of visual material, in pictures or objects before the pupils, used in close conjunction with carefully controlled utterances in the language that relate to the visual material. For example, a picture of a red house is flashed on to a screen by means of a film-strip or slide projector and at the same time a recorded voice from a tape-recorder is heard to say, *La maison est rouge*. The next picture, which follows after a few seconds shows a close-up of the front door, and the words are heard, *La porte est bleue*. In this way we can proceed through a complete course of many lessons, in which various items of lexis and grammar are systematically presented and thoroughly drilled. The picture is always there to convey the meaning and to provide a centre of attention, while the recorded voice gives the correct form of the utterance and the correct pronunciation and intonation. Actually, such a course is simply using mechanical devices to do what many teachers have done for years. Comenius, in the seventeenth century, devised a means of teaching Latin through a vast series of pictures, each related to certain words and phrases. Frequently teachers have held an object in front of a class and said, *Voici un livre. Qu'est-ce que c'est? . . . J'ouvre le livre. Qu'est-ce que je fais?* and so on. A teacher has often sketched a drawing on the blackboard to illustrate a phrase, or used a poster as a basis for conversational work. Modern teaching aids, however, provide the possibility of a much fuller and wider visual presentation than the teacher's ingenuity could ever produce previously. Slides, film-strips, flannelgraph, film and other aids, can bring into the classroom a representation of virtually all the objects, situations and actions of normal everyday life. The presentation can also be carefully controlled and graded, so that there is a systematic progression from one point to another. The recorded voice can also provide a nearly perfect and untiring model of speech for the pupils.

The various aids can be used in different ways and in different combinations. The co-ordination of tape-recorder and film-strip projector is a common and very satisfactory method of audio-visual presentation. But many teachers prefer slides to film-strips, as one can then revert more easily to any particular frame. Recordings on disc replace the tape in some courses, but the record-player cannot be stopped and started so readily as the tape-recorder, nor is it really practicable to put the needle down at a particular point on the record. In some courses a flannelgraph is used for the visual presentation, which gives maximum flexibility to the teacher in the construction of pictures. At the other extreme, a cine-film or television programme can provide the full sequence of pictures without any teacher participation. The advantage of a moving picture is very considerable in teaching linguistic features that relate to a series of events. In its simplest form, however, the visual element may be no more than the illustrations in a book. The oral element can be the teacher's live voice speaking about the pictures, rather than any recorded voice.

Certain important principles underlie the conception of an audio-visual course. In the first place the pictures do more than convey the meaning of the words. In fact in many cases they do not do this particularly well. What they do achieve is to set language in a situation, to provide language with its vital contextualisation which we considered in Chapter 3. In grammar-book language learning it is tacitly assumed that the pupil can make the enormous mental exertion of visualising every situation implied in the foreign words whose meaning he only imperfectly grasps. In an audio-visual course the situation is provided by the visual element.

It is thus possible to teach a language by such a method without reference to writing at all. All the problems of the written language, its often inconsistent and confusing orthography, those grammatical agreements which occur only in writing, and so on, can be eliminated entirely. In an earlier chapter we considered how adults often want to write, or see

73

written, every new linguistic form that they hear. But there may be situations in which it is almost impossible to do this, for example in teaching very young children, or in teaching a language, such as Chinese, that has a particularly difficult kind of graphic notation.

The combination of visual and aural presentation is likely to make a deeper impression on the pupil than could normally be achieved by conventional textbook teaching. The brightly lit screen is a centre of attention and interest and helps to ensure that everybody in the class is concentrating on the matter in hand. It must not be assumed, however, that an audio-visual course will necessarily appeal to children in schools. One can become bored with anything. If an audio-visual course is badly handled, so that pupils fail to grasp the meaning of the material presented to them, they will lose interest and begin to dislike the work. The recorded utterances on the tape are replayed with unfailing regularity; the tape goes on and on, untiring and relentless, so that the class has to work steadily and attentively to keep pace with it. This is particularly so when oral responses are required to the utterances on the tape. On the one hand there is a great advantage in this compulsion to work at the speed of the machine. But on the other hand there may be a tendency to monotony and fatigue as the tape continues its untiring series of statements or questions.

A final and most important advantage of courses of this kind is that they offer the possibility of systematic presentation and thorough drilling. Not only can vocabulary be limited and graded, but structures can be presented in the logical order, and, when introduced, a new structure can be carefully practised so that it becomes well established in the mind. All this can be well designed in a course that uses audio-visual devices.

Audio-lingual Courses

It is difficult to make any rigid distinction between 'audio-visual' courses and 'audio-lingual' courses, and indeed for a good number of courses both terms would be appropriate. It is not intended here to define these terms, but simply to give the reader some idea of what these expressions mean to those who use and hear them. Other expressions could equally well be used to describe the same things, and it would not be essential to choose terms which imply a distinction between 'audio-visual' on the one hand and 'audio-lingual' on the other. But as these terms are in use we might as well keep to them; the essential is, of course, to understand what we are talking about.

An audio-lingual course is designed to teach the spoken language and to give plenty of practice in its use. It makes extensive use of recordings in the language, which are usually of native speakers' voices. It need not have the well-defined visual element that is a vital part of an audio-visual course, but normally a textbook is supplied to each pupil, which may be extensively illustrated. Often the pupils are required to follow the textbook while listening to the recording. They have to make oral responses to utterances in the recorded course by repeating phrases, answering questions or changing sentences in some way. There is opportunity here for pattern practice to be used, and this work can be done either in a normal classroom equipped with a tape-recorder or in a language laboratory. As in the case of audio-visual courses a great deal of follow-up work is done by the teacher without the mechanical equipment, though he may in this follow-up use the textbook considerably.

A textbook for an audio-lingual course is very different from a textbook of the type with which we have become so familiar in Britain over the last fifty years or so. Until recently the general design of languages textbooks has remained constant since the time of the Direct Methodists. Textbooks of this traditional kind contain (a) passages in the language for reading and study, (b) explanations of grammar and usage, and (c) exercises to be worked in writing or sometimes orally. To these elements may be added other features, such as word lists or suggestions for games and songs. An audio-lingual course book, however, is not designed at all for the study of grammar in the abstract or for copious written exercises, nor does it present in the early stages considerable passages of continuous prose. It usually contains dialogues, which present the words and structures to be learned, and which set this material in a real situation. Developing this material there is then extensive provision for aural pattern practice and for question-and-answer activities. This work occupies a very important place in an audio-lingual course. All the time the stress is not put on abstract knowledge of the grammar of the written language, but on ability to manipulate the structures of the spoken language. Other conversations may be added to develop the original dialogue still further, and various other oral activities may be suggested.

Ideally such courses and such methods should be based on the careful scientific analysis of the contrasts between the learner's language and the target language. It is evident that a great deal of work is necessary to prepare the linguistic material of the course. This involves not only a careful grading of lexis and a logical order in the presentation of grammar, but also a comparison of structure in the two languages concerned, so that in the pattern practice particular emphasis is put on those features of structure which are likely to offer most difficulty.

Structure and Situation

In compiling any audio-visual or audio-lingual course the authors will be obliged to face a basic matter of principle which needs to be settled before the construction of the course can proceed. It is possible to start with the simplest linguistic structures of the language and drill these one by one, proceeding always from one structure to the next. One might start with the structure which involves only subject and verb; then one could go on to the structure involving subject, verb and complement; thirdly, one might take the interrogative or negative form of this; and so on. The choice of structures would depend on the nature of the language in question, but the course would be built up largely on a sequence of structures. Alternatively, one might start with the simplest possible situation in which language is used. This might be a meeting of two persons in the street who exchange common greetings.

One would build up a brief dialogue for such a situation, and then thoroughly drill the utterances of that dialogue. The course would then proceed to another situation, slightly different or slightly less simple, and so new types of sentence would be introduced and gradually learned. Now each of these two methods of designing a course can be justified, because on the one hand the language learner has got to acquire the facility for using certain structures, and on the other hand he has got to be able to use his linguistic knowledge in a situation.

We might conclude that the right method would be to learn a structure first and then apply that structure to a situation. But this would involve making an unreal abstraction of the structure in the first place. No utterance has significance unless it is related to a situation, and we have no wish to teach meaningless sentences, even if that were possible. Language learning that isolates structure too much from situation can become hopelessly dull and monotonous. The endless repetition of sentences illustrating a certain pattern or structure can become as soul-destroying as any grammar-grind.

If we revert to a completely situational approach we shall greatly enliven the interest of the subject-matter. Bright and breezy conversations about everyday matters in simple but idiomatic language can be very entertaining. But we shall soon find that we are involved in embarrassing complications of structure, which should really be kept for a later stage of the course. It is extremely difficult to limit dialogues to precisely those elements of structure which we wish to include.

Here then is the problem that every course writer must face. Almost certainly there will need to be a blend of the two possible approaches. It is possible to start with a simple situation and its appropriate dialogue and then to extract the desired structures from the dialogue and drill them. The next unit of the course would start with another dialogue and and so on. This plan has much to commend it, but it may lead to structures and idioms being introduced in the dialogues which we have not time adequately to drill in the practice that follows. An alternative solution is to choose a few simple structures which can easily be built into the dialogue of a situation. We have the situation in mind from the start and in our structure drills we are working towards it. But if the dialogue is then limited to the structures learned it may be rather stilted and lifeless. As we shall see in examining courses, some tend to one kind of solution to this problem, some tend to another.

Some Courses

When NATO established its headquarters in France shortly after World War II, an interesting language teaching problem arose. Military personnel of fourteen different countries, speaking nine different languages among themselves, were stationed for a considerable period in France and needed a working knowledge of spoken French. As these would-be students had no common language used by them all, traditional classroom methods were of no avail. Tape-recorders became available for teaching purposes, and V. Kameneff, an able linguist, teacher and artist, who had been experimenting since 1943 with teaching methods, set to work in producing what was in effect an audio-visual French course. His cartoons were photographed on 35mm film and projected before the class in conjunction with tape-recordings. In cooperation with an American colleague, Kameneff adapted his course for the children of the foreign personnel at SHAPE in 1952-53. This course was tried out at Beeston, Nottingham in 1956-57, and from 1958 onwards it was used at East Ham under the direction of S. R. Ingram. The work at East Ham attracted very considerable attention. Mr Ingram and a colleague wrote a number of articles about the use of the course, notably in *Modern Languages* and in *Visual Education,* as well as lecturing and demonstrating in various parts of the country. The course, now known as the *Tavor French Course,* was distributed commercially by the Educational Foundation for Visual Aids, and began to be used in a number of schools of various kinds from about 1960 onwards.

In the *cours préliminaire* each lesson unit is divided into four parts and includes enough material for at least a week's work. The first part provides a series of pictures with utterances appropriate to them given on the tape in English. The second part gives the same pictures with the utterances in French. The third part is a repetition of the second part, but with pauses between the utterances during which the class is required to repeat; each utterance is given three times on the tape. In the final part there are questions on the same material which are to be answered orally by the pupils. The whole approach is oral and no written work need be done at all in the early stages of the course. The *cours préliminaire,* subdivided into three parts, provides more than enough work for the first year of a secondary school course. The next part of the course, called *premier degré,* is designed in a similar way, but introduces the pupil to a systematic study of grammar and grammatical forms by means of an oral approach. Provision is also made at this stage for written work. The course has been used successfully both in the early forms of secondary schools and in the nine to eleven year age range in primary schools. Most teachers who have used the course like it very much, but when they have opportunity to compare it in detail with other courses they often become more critical. Generally speaking the design of the course is structural rather than situational, and the lack of a story in the lessons is a drawback, especially with young pupils. The fact that each utterance is given three times in section three of each lesson is often criticised for tending to monotony; it is an example of how a structural course can be somewhat dull. For all this the course has some excellent qualities and has met with a good deal of success.

We have already mentioned that linguistic research in France, conducted under Professor Gougenheim, had produced *Le Français Fondamental.* Using this as a linguistic basis, linguists and teachers at the research centre established in 1952 at Saint-Cloud, known as the *Centre de Recherches et d'Études pour la Diffusion du Français,* worked on the production of an audio-visual French course for adults. Most of the work on this was done in the late 1950s and the course, entitled *Voix et Images de France,* became available in Britain, distributed by Harrap, soon after *Tavor.* For several years the two courses were keen rivals in this country and many comparisons were made between them. The authors of the CREDIF course insisted that before any teacher used *Voix et Images de France* he must follow an approved course in audio-visual methods. This hampered distribution of the course for some time and *Tavor* became more widely known. Gradually, however, the qualities of the CREDIF course became apparent and many schools and colleges began to use it.

The first part of this course, which like *Tavor* makes use of film-strips and tape-recordings, is divided into thirty-two lessons, each consisting of the lesson itself, a section called *mécanisme,* and a phonetic exercise. The first section of the lesson consists of a little incident or story that is related in the pictures of the film-strip, while the appropriate utterances of the persons involved are heard from the tape. This is clearly a situational approach. The vocabulary used is that of *Le Français Fondamental,* and the dialogue is similar to that which one hears in ordinary everyday French conversation. The authors say that the course should be entirely oral for the first sixty hours of class work; only after this much oral work has been done should the written language be introduced. The section of the lesson that is called *mécanisme,* is again the dialogue of an incident or situation, but this time arranged in such a way as to give practice in the use of a particular point of grammar. The course is carefully designed to cover all the essential details of the grammar of *Le Français Fondamental,* but these are never presented formally. There is nothing in the nature of pattern practice, but copious explanations are given of how the teacher might exploit and develop the lesson. All this work is intended to grow from the dialogues and to result in a deeper knowledge of the forms and expressions used. There is no doubt that this is an exceedingly good course. Well used, it is more lively and more sophisticated than *Tavor,* but it is also certainly more demanding of the teacher. The second part of the course, called *deuxième degré,* has no visual element but consists mainly of recorded dialogues. It involves intensive oral study of a text and makes suggestions for both oral and written composition.

The CREDIF team also produced an entirely different audio-visual course, called *Bonjour Line,* which has been specially designed for children of eight to eleven years. Again based on *Le Français Fondamental, Bonjour Line* has twenty-eight lessons, each involving a film-strip and tape-recording. Each lesson presents an incident in a story that runs right through the course and which concerns the adventures of a group of children. Each lesson ends with the *jeu des questions,* which is a dialogue about the incident between a doll-pupil called Line and her teacher. The course, which again is situational, has great appeal for primary school children. As it is intended to be used with this younger age group, there are no specific plans for written work. This course has been very popular in primary schools in this country, both with pupils and teachers, and has done a great deal to assist the teaching of French to children of this age.

Both these CREDIF courses claim to be very carefully planned linguistically. There is no doubt that the planning is systematic, but it is difficult to discern exactly what is the linguistic system lying behind the courses and the planned progression in presentation of vocabulary and grammatical structures, unless the teacher has attended one of the training courses organised by CREDIF.

In 1962 an American audio-visual course on cine-film began to be distributed in this country by Harrap. This was the Heath de Rochemont *Parlons Français* course, which is very expensive and it is probably its high cost which has considerably limited its use in schools in Britain. It was originally intended as a French course for American elementary school classes where the teacher had almost no previous knowledge of the language. The sixty 16mm films of the course present to the pupils all the linguistic material that they need. The teacher is expected to conduct follow-up lessons based on the films that have been shown, so that he is in effect learning with the class. It can be expected that the work would go much better when the teacher is fluent in French. Each film is in colour and runs for about fifteen minutes. A teacher, Mrs Anne Slack, herself a native French speaker, appears on the screen and leads the class in repetitive drills, in learning the dialogue of short incidents or sketches, which are also shown on the screen, and in learning songs. The production is lavish and colourful, and while most of the action takes place in the studio, there are also some very fine shots in France itself. Once the film has started the teacher cannot intervene and he has to leave the teaching to Mrs Slack and the film. This limitation, which the teacher must accept, is largely compensated for by the colourful and lively way in which the linguistic subject matter is presented in the films.

For many years there have been available for language teaching films which provide additional interest and background information about the land where the language is spoken. The film is an admirable medium for this purpose, and many more films of this kind are now available. What is distinctive about the *Parlons Français* course is that the films are not merely supplementary, but form the essential core of the language teaching work. They set out to teach the elements of the language to young children who are beginners. Most other language films have been intended for those who have already a considerable knowledge of the language. This course makes clear what the great possibilities of this medium are. A major difficulty, however, is to obtain really clear voice reproduction with normal film projection. Sometimes in schools the voice from the sound track is very muffled and nearly drowned by the whirr of the projector. When the sound is produced with greater clarity and when projectors become silent, we may hope that this audio-visual medium will become much more effective in language teaching.

The B.B.C. has produced an audio-visual French course, *French for Beginners,* of which the audio element has to be recorded on tape by schools from a weekly broadcast. The film-strips have to be purchased, but as the sound is received over the air the financial outlay for any school is considerably less than in the case of other courses. This is perhaps one of the main attractions of this course, which since it first became available in the autumn of 1964, has been popular in schools. It is largely situational and concentrates on the everyday use of the spoken language. Each lesson is divided into three sections. The first of these presents the essential linguistic material by means of a short scene involving a few characters, some of whom reappear throughout the course. The second section provides questions and answers on this material, and the third is a dramatic scene which expands the material of the first section. The quality of the artist's work in drawing the pictures for the film-strips has been a good deal criticised, but the course appeals to pupils nevertheless. It is intended for secondary school beginners.

En Avant, the French course which is being produced by the Nuffield Foundation Foreign Languages Teaching Materials Project,[1] does not limit itself to any one visual medium. The first stage of this course, which became available commercially in 1966, uses mainly figurines, which can be attached to a sheet of flannel or to a magnetic board, and tape-recordings. These figurines are in colour, which adds considerably to the interest and appeal. The second stage of the Nuffield course utilizes coloured posters and reading cards, for it is in this stage that the written language is to be presented to the pupils. Later stages of the course make use of the film-strip and other means of visual presentation, including films, as may be considered appropriate. An outstanding feature of this course is that it is based on careful and thorough experiment. Produced by a team of workers including a linguist, a teacher, a native speaker and an artist, the first stage of the course was tried out in a limited number of schools before it was supplied to the primary schools of the Schools Council's pilot scheme. Only after further modification resulting from this second testing, has it been released to the public. There is no doubt that the production of any such course demands both teamwork and thorough experiment. Notes are supplied for the teacher, but he is left largely free to design his lessons as he thinks best and to use the method he prefers. He may mix the ingredients provided in whatever way he chooses and may introduce additional vocabulary if he wishes to do so. Only he must abide by the order of lesson units and he must not introduce new

[1] See pp. 162-4.

linguistic structures in addition to those given in the course. This course is to provide for French teaching from the age of eight to the age of thirteen, thereby seeking to bridge the gap between enterprising work in the primary school and language teaching in the early years of the secondary school.

Among the various audio-visual courses now available, *Longmans Audio-Visual French,* by S. Moore and A. L. Antrobus, is probably the first course of its kind to be devised specifically for secondary school pupils in Britain. Using film-strips, tapes and flashcards, as well as books, it will provide a full five-year course leading to Ordinary level, the first stage of which was published in the summer of 1966. After the teacher has used the first two stages, he can, if he so wishes, follow an alternative version of the course that is particularly suitable for pupils working for C.S.E. The structures and the vocabulary presented in the course are based on *Le Français Fondamental,* and appear to be carefully graded throughout. The later stages of the course provide for aural comprehension and composition work, written composition work and for preparation for new types of examinations. It is also intended to produce a range of readers and other subsidiary material integrated with the course.

An example of a fully audio-lingual course is an American production supplied by Holt, Rinehart and Winston, Inc., of which the first-year course by Côté, Levy and O'Connor is entitled *Le Français: Écouter et Parler.*[1] This course involves textbooks, workbooks, flashcards, tests and recordings on disc and tape. The linguistic material is arranged in twenty units and five reading and review sections. Each unit consists of Basic Dialogue Sentences, which form the main element of the unit, followed by Question-Answer Practice, Pattern Practice and Conversations, which expand and develop the Basic Dialogue

[1] D. G. Côté, S. N. Levy, and P. O'Connor, *Le Français: Ecouter et Parler (Teacher's edition),* New York: Holt, Rinehart and Winston, Inc., 1962. This is the teacher's manual for the first year course. Pupil's books, recordings, flashcards, etc. are also available. The second year course is *Le Français: Parler et Lire* (1963), and the third year course is *Le Français: Parler, Lire et Ecrire* (1964).

Sentences. There is abundant material here for varied and copious oral work in class or in a language laboratory. The course is intended for young Americans of twelve to fifteen years of age who are beginning French, and the subject matter is often too sophisticated for English children of eleven or twelve. It would need a good deal of adaptation to be really suitable for an English secondary school. The first year of the course as the title suggests is concerned with the skills of aural comprehension and of expression in the spoken language. The second year's course, *Le Français: Parler et Lire,* places more emphasis on reading and writing, introduces more of French culture and begins the study of grammar through the formal analysis of already familiar grammatical patterns. The third year of the course, *Le Français: Parler, Lire et Ecrire,* carries these developments further still. What is most interesting for us here is that this is a new type of course, that breaks away from the set pattern of the traditional textbook. In fact, however, it gives so many detailed instructions to the teacher, that it might be found to hamper a really original teacher who had his own imaginative ideas about his teaching.

The same publishers supply courses of very similar design in both German and Spanish. These all have the disadvantage, however, that they are not specifically planned for British schools.

Let's Speak French,[1] by Pamela Symonds, is a course which is much more suitable for schools in Britain. It is perhaps the first course book to appear in this country which presents a fully audio-lingual approach. Like the American course we have just considered it has no formal presentation of grammar and no translation exercises in books one or two. Each chapter or unit starts with a page of pictures with a text related to the pictures printed on the page opposite. The pictures can also be obtained as wall charts and the linguistic material is available in recorded form on tape. Each unit of the course also has a good variety of oral exercises in the form of questions

[1] P. Symonds, *Let's Speak French,* Oxford University Press; Book I, 1962; Book II, 1963. Accompanying tape-recordings and pictures can be obtained from the Tutor Tape Company Ltd., 2 Replingham Road, London S.W. 18.

about the pictures and the text, to which answers are sometimes suggested. Some other oral exercises occur, as well as dialogues for use in class. There is no pattern exercise in this course, but it does appear to be built up as a logical progression of structures to be learned. These, however, are drilled by the question-and-answer method, rather than by pattern practice. In the latter part of book one and throughout book two, most chapters present an incident or anecdote from French family life, which provides more interest and helps to enliven the question-and-answer drills.

These two books provide work for the first two years of the secondary school course. A series of audio-visual readers, under the general title *Let's Read French,* are being produced as a sequel and could be used in the third and fourth years. Each reader provides a story either in abbreviated audio-visual form, or as a printed text accompanied by photographs reproduced in the book itself. The full text is available on tape. If we can judge the series from the first reader, *Gérard Vernier,* which has already appeared, it seems that the subject matter is admirably suited to the tastes and interests of young people in their early teens. Each reader provides enough material for one term's work and leaves the teacher a great deal of liberty for putting more or less emphasis on the visual element according to the capacity of the class.

Audio-lingual courses that have become well known in this country are the *A-L M* courses[1] in French, German, Italian, Russian and Spanish. These American courses are usually employed in schools where a language laboratory is available, but they are really courses that can be used equally well in a normal classroom equipped with a tape-recorder. Each unit of these courses starts with a dialogue and is followed by pattern practice and other oral drills designed to develop a practical knowledge of grammatical structures and a facility for using them. The *A-L M* courses have the same general shape as *Le Français: Écouter et Parler.* No reading or writing is involved in the early stages of Level One, but a supplement is provided

---

[1] *A-L M* (Audio-Lingual Materials), published by Rupert Hart-Davis, 36 Soho Square, London W.1.

for the teacher's guidance in making the transition to
of reading and written work.[1]

Experience in the Schools

This brief survey of some of the audio-visual and audio
courses available in this country is not intended to
haustive; indeed a number of excellent courses have no
mentioned for reasons of space alone. But some of th
known have been included, and an attempt has been ma
convey something of the nature and the range of these co
As with course books of the traditional kind, these courses
provide ideas to the teacher. Here and there he will
activities or exercises that he would like to incorporate
his own system of teaching. It is often difficult to find a rea
made course that suits the particular circumstances of any
particular class and the inclinations and character of
individual teacher. As more courses become available, the
will be more choice. But still many more courses are neede
especially in languages other than French.

Where schools have adopted an audio-visual course this ha
generally speaking been done in one of two possible ways
Either the school has committed itself fully to one course, such
as *Tavor* or *Voix et Images de France,* and used that course
almost exclusively in the first year or two of the secondary
school, or else the audio-visual course has been taken up from
time to time as an adjunct to the main course of language
teaching. In the second case the audio-visual course has been
employed in much the same way as a reader might be used, or
as the B.B.C. sound programmes are intended to be used. In
many cases this has been the attitude of primary school teachers
to the audio-visual courses. When the teacher has mapped out
a clear course of his own, and has really integrated the audio-

[1] Other audio-visual French courses are described and reviewed in
*Audio-Visual French Courses for Primary Schools—An annotated Biblio-
graphy,* published for the Nuffield Foreign Languages Teaching Materials
Project by E. J. Arnold and Sons, Butterley Street, Leeds 10. A useful list
of such courses in various languages is also issued by the National Committee for Audio-Visual Aids in Education, entitled *Audio-Visual Materials
for Modern Languages.*

visual work into this course, this system can work very well. There are audio-visual aids that are intended to be used in precisely this way, as an adjunct of the main course. They are *Macmillan Cineloops,* devised by G. Fleming, and there are twelve of them for French teaching. They are cassette-loading film-loops for an 800E projector, and each depicts an incident in the life of the Carré family. The teacher can provide his own commentary or make use of tapes which are available for approximate synchronisation with the film-loops. This aid provides a moving picture without the usual high costs of conventional films. It is not a complete course, and the work with the film-loops needs to be carefully integrated with the regular language teaching.

If on the other hand extracts from a full audio-visual course are used occasionally with a class there are grave dangers. If the use of film-strip projector and tape-recorder is just a pleasant relaxation for an afternoon, and is felt to be such by the pupils, then the real advantage of the carefully planned audio-visual course is lost altogether. A course involving a steady progression from structure to structure, from point to point in grammar, and introducing vocabulary according to a systematised plan, is clearly to be taken seriously and worked through in the way that the author suggested.

When teachers have made an audio-visual course the main pillar and stay of the language learning task, some very interesting results have arisen. It is necessary to plan a regular weekly or fortnightly cycle of lessons. One school spends a fortnight on each lesson unit of the audio-visual course. There are five French periods in each week, and these in the first week of the fortnight are made up as follows: one audio-visual period in which the new lesson unit is introduced, two follow-up lessons in which the film-strip may be used, but not the tape-recording, and then two more audio-visual periods in which the class sees and hears the whole lesson again. The second week of the fortnight is devoted to consolidating the work of the previous week and to developing reading and written work. Another school, using the same course, does not keep to a rigid weekly programme, but generally follows

this sequence of periods for each lesson of the course: an audio-visual period to introduce each lesson unit, one or two follow-up periods, another fully audio-visual period, and then one or two more for follow-up. A third school has no plan laid down, and each of the five teachers using the audio-visual course are free to follow whatever sequence of teaching periods they wish to. These three examples show the kind of arrangements that may arise.

If the pupils have no textbook in their hands and if written work is delayed for too long there is a real danger that pupils may find something rather bewildering about the work. Even a pupil who is making satisfactory progress may find he has no means of taking stock of what he has learned, no point of reference to tell him how far he has progressed through the course, and perhaps no yard-stick by which to measure his achievement. He may have a sense of being 'lost', and consequently interest may fail. This is one of the reasons why most schools prefer to introduce written work at a fairly early point in the secondary school course. But even if written and oral work are proceeding together, new words and phrases are usually introduced in oral work and thoroughly learned in speech before they are met in print or in writing.

When a certain body of linguistic material—words, phrases and sentences—has been learned by the class orally, the first step in the transition to written work is for the pupils to see this material printed or written. Reading is the first activity that relates to the written language. Writing follows this; so that when the pupils have a certain visual acquaintance with the material the teacher then proceeds to ask them to copy the words and sentences into their own exercise books. This may appear too simple, but it is vital that the transition from oral work to written work should be gradual and should not pose problems at any stage. The objective is that acquaintance with the written language should never disturb the aural image that each pupil should have formed in his mind of every word and phrase. He should only write down sentences that he can say accurately. The next step, after copying, can be dictation, an exercise which closely relates the spoken and written modes.

Only when the simple aspects of written work have been mastered does the teacher ask the pupils to tackle more difficult written exercises, such as completing unfinished sentences or answering questions.

One aim of written work is to consolidate a knowledge of the written forms, and thus it is a support to reading. A person who can write in a language must of necessity have the capacity to read those same written forms. Reading precedes writing in language learning, but exercises in writing can consolidate the knowledge necessary for reading. But the ultimate objective of written work is free expression in the written mode of the language. All activities in written work should be planned with free composition in view. Oral composition can lead towards this also. Indeed it would be quite unsound to expect any pupil to write down anything that he cannot say. An audio-lingual course will involve oral composition at some point. This may be the description of a picture, perhaps one frame from the film-strip of an audio-visual course, or a situation that the pupil himself sets out on the flannelgraph. When a pupil can describe such a picture with some ease in spoken language, and when he has also had practice in copying out the words and phrases that he uses for this description or practice in taking them down in a dictation, then, and only then, can we reasonably expect him to write down his description of the picture as a free composition.

Schools using audio-visual and audio-lingual courses are working along these lines. We should not expect sensational changes in the achievement of pupils, because the improvement of language teaching is, like language learning itself, a long and hard process. But it is already clear that these new methods enable some pupils to speak a foreign language who would never have made any real progress before. It is also evident that the whole attitude to language takes on a more lively character in a class using these new methods. Such methods are not without their dangers, as we have seen, but they must ultimately lead more surely to the objective of effective oral communication in the foreign language.

Programmed Learning

In recent years a good deal of publicity has been given to teaching machines and to the kind of instruction associated with such machines, which is generally called *programmed learning*. We need now to examine the contribution that programmed learning can make to language learning, and to consider whether teaching machines can be useful to the language teacher. We do not regard the tape-recorder, the film-strip projector and the cine-projector as teaching machines, for this latter term is usually reserved for machines that provide for programmed learning.

The first characteristic of programmed learning is that the subject-matter to be taught is divided up into the smallest possible items of information, each item consisting of only one or two sentences. These items are then presented to the pupil one by one in a sequential order so that they build up to a coherent body of subject-matter. But as each item is presented the pupil's understanding of it is tested, so as to ensure that he follows every step in the programme as it proceeds. An example will make this clear. What follows is taken from the first page of *A Programmed German Grammar* by A. K. Tyrer. Each of the seven items of subject-matter in this example is called a *frame*. To each frame the pupil is required to give a response which can only be right or wrong. When the pupil has constructed his response he turns the page of his book, or moves down a shield, or turns a knob on his machine, and thus reveals the correct response. In this case the correct responses are printed in a column on the left, opposite the next frame. The pupil knows at once whether he is right or wrong. He then proceeds to the next frame.

GENDER

1

In English, nouns which denote male creatures are sometimes said to be of the MASCULINE GENDER. Which of the following words is of the masculine gender?
Man/woman/house.

	GENDER
	2
Man	Similarly, *boy* is of the masculine ——.
	3
gender	*Man, boy, widower* are all of the —— gender.
	4
masculine	Nouns which denote female creatures are said to be of the FEMININE GENDER. Which of the following words is of the feminine gender? *Man/woman/house.*
	5
woman	Similarly, *girl* is of the —— gender.
	6
feminine	Nouns which denote creatures or things which are neither of the masculine nor the feminine gender are said to be of the NEUTER GENDER. ('Neuter' is another word for 'neither'). Which of the following is of the neuter gender? *Man/woman/house.*
	7
house	Similarly, *table* is of the —— gender.
neuter[1]	

Each frame presents only a very small item of new knowledge. The response required of the pupil is as simple as possible and therefore he usually gets his responses right. This technique of encouraging the pupil by telling him as often as possible that his response is correct is called *reinforcement*. Many pupils could go through a programme working only every other frame and yet understand the subject matter. The intentional break-up of the material into very small items ensures that it is not only understood but *overlearned*.

This type of programme is usually associated with B. F. Skinner, Professor of Psychology at Harvard, and is often called a *linear* programme. Another type of programme is the *branching* type, which has been developed by Norman Crowder of the Educational Science Division of U.S. Industries, Inc. In a branching programme information is presented in larger units of a paragraph or a page. Having read this material the pupil is required to answer a question on it by choosing one of a number of suggested answers. If he chooses the right

---

[1] A. K. Tyrer, *A Programmed German Grammar*, Methuen, 1965, p. 17.

answer he proceeds to the next frame in the programme. If he chooses a wrong answer he is branched to a frame that explains to him why his answer was wrong and gives him another chance to understand. This type of programme can be presented on an electronic teaching machine, which shows the frame on a small illuminated screen and requires the pupil to select his answer by pressing the appropriate button.[1]

Each type of programme can however be presented in textbook form. In the case of a linear programme in a textbook, the pupil is required to cover the answers, which are printed on one side of the page, with a shield, and to uncover them one by one as he proceeds. A branching programme can be printed in a *scrambled* textbook, in which each frame appears on a separate page, and the pupil is directed from one page to another according to the nature of his replies.

It might appear that programmed learning is mainly concerned with imparting information, rather than with fostering skills. If we wish to teach a certain body of facts, a carefully prepared programme can be a great help. A course about language, which is mainly concerned with facts, can fairly easily be programmed as the above example shows. We can see in this example that the responses required involve very largely the correct use of certain semi-technical words. Extending this procedure to the learning of vocabulary, a programme could be devised, solely in the foreign language, that aimed at presenting new lexical items and at getting the pupil to use these items correctly in his responses. Programming could then be used not only for presenting the facts of grammar or of phonetics, but also for teaching vocabulary.

In this sense the programme is doing more than imparting facts. It is requiring certain behaviour in the use of vocabulary. Some psychologists would maintain that a programme can be devised to teach anything, provided the desired terminal behaviour can be defined. This means that if we can define the use of words that we wish to teach, a programme can be drawn

---

[1] Such a machine available in the U.K. is the Autotutor Mark II Teaching Machine, made by U.S. Industries Inc. Great Britain Ltd., 1-5 New Bond Street, London, W.1.

up that not only presents vocabulary, but teaches how to use it. The programme induces certain terminal linguistic behaviour in the use of words. It is then not only imparting information, but it is teaching a skill.

Language programmes have been designed along these lines, but have the disadvantage of mixing the mother tongue and the target language. An even more serious drawback is that such a programme is teaching only the written language, and cannot teach pronunciation or speech skills. If it is simply a reading knowledge of the language that is required, then there are some possibilities in programmes that mingle the two languages. H. H. Schaefer, of Pittsburg University, has developed a type of programme which takes sentences in the mother tongue and substitutes a word here and there in the target language. Gradually vocabulary and even grammar can be taught by this system. The *Prentice-Hall Programmed Reading French Series,* edited by J. P. Ebacher, takes a French text and supplies in interlinear type the meanings of words which are likely to be unknown to an English-speaking reader. As the reader proceeds, more and more words are learned and less and less interlinear props are required.

These systems may teach the skills of silent reading, but do not teach speech. If we wish to teach the skills of speech, as indeed we do, we need to arrange for a tape-recorder to work in conjunction with the programmed textbook or the teaching machine. At least one make of teaching machine supplied in this country provides for this possibility,[1] and no doubt this could be used for language teaching. Examples occurring on the printed frame could also be heard from the tape, and the pupil would be required to repeat or respond orally to the utterances he heard. This is virtually an extension of language laboratory work, which we are going to consider in Chapter 6. In a language laboratory we are concerned with spoken language and with fostering speech skills.

It is most valuable to notice here that the principles of Skinnerian programming can be well applied in language

[1] This is the Empirical Tutor, supplied by Lamson Technical Products Ltd., Linmoor Works, Hillborough, Herne Bay, Kent.

laboratory courses. A constructed response is required from the pupil, and by giving the correct response on the master track of the tape, immediate reinforcement is provided. Repeated examples ensure overlearning of linguistic features, and subject matter is learned in very small items, which build up to one coherent body of knowledge and skills. It is then in the language laboratory and in the audio-lingual courses providing language laboratory exercises that programmed learning has its principal application to language teaching.[1]

The application of programming to language learning in a laboratory has been developed in a remarkable way by Dr F. Rand Morton working at the universities of Harvard, Berkeley and Michigan. One of his programmes is divided into four major phases. The first of these, which he calls *phonemetization*, aims at teaching the pupil to discriminate accurately between the sounds of the target language and those of his mother tongue and between different sounds in the target language. The pupil says nothing in this phase, which may last for fifty hours of learning time, but simply builds up an instinctive response system to the foreign sounds. In the next phase, that of *vocalization*, he begins to make these sounds himself, and his ear has by this time been so well trained that he can detect his own errors of pronunciation when he hears his own recorded efforts played back from the tape. In the third phase, the phase of *acoustic signifiers*, the pupils learn the structures of the language by a series of drills which are rather similar to pattern practice, but at this stage he is not aware of meaning. The final phase is that of *lexical orientation*. Here the pupil is taught meaning by what is virtually an audio-visual course. The pupil follows stories, the meaning of which is made clear by a series of pictures.

Dr Morton's programme, which on average will take the pupil 200 hours to work, aims at producing as its terminal behaviour the speech that would be normal in an eight-year-old

[1] For further information on this subject see R. Lado, *Language Teaching*, chapter 19; also R. Goodman, *Programmed Learning and Teaching Machines—an Introduction*, English Universities Press, 1963; and M. Goldsmith, ed., *Mechanisation in the Classroom: an introduction to teaching machines and programmed learning*, Souvenir Press, 1963.

native speaker. Such a system would need to be judged ultimately on the results it produces. It may well be that the best results in language laboratory work will be achieved by programmes of this kind. In any case there is here a suggestion of some of the possibilities that may result from the union of the psychological principles of programming and the use of technological aids for recording speech.[1]

Radio and Television

The use of radio programmes in language teaching is hardly a new technique. For many years now the B.B.C. has provided language broadcasts for schools, which in their own way have been excellent. These broadcasts do not, however, attempt to provide in themselves a complete course, but they can enrich the normal classroom teaching in two ways. First, they provide a wider experience in the language; the pupils listening to the broadcast hear a wider range of voices speaking the foreign language than can normally be heard in school, and these voices are heard, too, in situations that it is difficult to stimulate in the classroom. Second, these broadcasts present a good deal of background information about France or Germany, and about the lives of people in those countries.

The value of these broadcasts has been enormously increased for schoolteachers by the possibility of recording broadcasts on tape. It is now legally permissible to record a broadcast on tape, provided the recording is used for educational purposes, and provided it is erased or disposed of at the end of the school year. This facility enables timetable difficulties to be resolved and the tape can be used whenever it is required, regardless of the time at which the original broadcast was made. The taped version can also be stopped, restarted or replayed as the teacher may wish, which gives much greater flexibility to the teacher using the broadcast in his lesson.

Since 1954 the B.B.C. has developed broadcast language courses for the general listening public in a number of

[1] A fuller account of one of Morton's courses and of Schaefer's programmes is given in B. Dutton, 'Linguistics and Programmed Instruction in Modern Language Teaching' in *Guide to Modern Language Teaching*, ed. B. Dutton, Cassell, 1965.

European languages. These courses, which operate in French, Russian, Spanish, Italian and German, are complete in themselves and are not supplementary to a school course, as the school broadcasts are. They therefore have to be designed to cover all aspects of the language and to give adequate explanation of the linguistic material presented and full practice in its use. It is of course assumed that the serious listener will do considerable work on his own in addition to listening times. Such courses offer considerable possibilities, since they can be carefully planned and produced by expert linguists and teachers, and since the resources of a broadcasting studio are considerably greater than the facilities available in the average classroom. They have however the grave disadvantage of a lack of feedback from student to teacher and of the virtual impossibility for the student of getting his efforts corrected by the teacher.

The advent of television has opened up fresh possibilities for language teaching. Some of the first language television programmes for schools in this country followed the principles of the well-established sound programmes, and sought on the one hand to provide a wider experience in the language and on the other to present something of the foreign nation's culture and way of life. This has been the general character of the ITA programmes, *Notre Ville,* 11 *Rue de la Gare* and *Ici la France*. It is at once clear that this audio-visual medium has enormous possibilities. A class can be shown scenes of French life taking place in France and can hear the language in everyday use in situations that are portrayed on the screen. But a TV programme of this kind is not automatically effective. Sound reception must be virtually flawless, that is to say, of a far higher standard than is normally necessary, otherwise the main value of the programme is lost. A great deal of work is called for on the part of both teacher and class to get the maximum benefit from such programmes.

As television can provide a truly audio-visual course, it offers greater possibilities for a complete language course than does sound alone. Language can be set in situations and meaning can be conveyed by the pictures on the screen; in fact

97

almost all that we have said in favour of audio-visual courses applies to TV. It is hardly surprising that B.B.C. television courses for beginners in a language, such as *Parliamo Italiano* and *Komm Mit! Wir Sprechen Deutsch,* have met with conspicuous success. The serious disadvantage in the lack of feedback, which we have noted in connection with sound broadcasts, still remains, but the visual element is such an advantage that it does much to help the student over these difficulties. As we might expect, these courses are very largely of the situational type, since the presentation of a real situation is the outstanding contribution that the medium has to make. Structure drills can however be brought in and can be followed up by the student in his private work with the accompanying booklet.

We may wonder what is to be the place of television language teaching in schools in Britain in the next few years. Clearly programmes of the enrichment type have a great deal to offer and could become an almost essential part of language teaching. Language teachers throughout the country should be far more vociferous in demanding the types of programme that they really need. Problems for those who organise and produce the programmes are very considerable, as there is no general agreement in any detail about what vocabulary or sentence structures are appropriate for any particular stage in the course, as there will be much difference of opinion about the best subject matter, and as timetable problems are almost insoluble. But the more teachers ask for what they want, the more they are likely to get it.

A teacher using a television programme with his class is obliged to stand back until the programme is ended. He cannot usually intervene to explain a point, to answer a question or to reinforce something in the programme. His place may be taken for the time being by a screen teacher, such as Anne Slack in *Parlons Français.* The screen teacher may ask for class participation in various ways, usually in simply asking for repetitions by the class of certain phrases or sentences. There can however be no immediate feedback to the screen teacher, who therefore cannot adapt his teaching to the reactions of the class or the response of individual pupils. On the other hand each pupil watching the screen has the impression that the screen teacher is looking directly at him and giving him almost individual tuition. When the programme is over, the normal teacher of the class will be obliged in follow-up work to adopt something very similar to the methods of the screen teacher. Indeed the teacher must be prepared to accept the methods of the programme and model his own follow-up work very closely on this. Experienced teachers may not find this easy, though teachers with little experience, or imperfect knowledge of the language, may be very glad to have a model. There can of course be feedback to the live teacher in the classroom. He may note persistent errors in the class chorus repetitions during the watching of the programme, and these he will seek to correct in follow-up work.

A TV language programme can go further in pupil participation. Sometimes one character in a sketch may at some point in the programme come forward to the camera and speak directly to the class or ask the class to repeat a phrase or give other responses. After the showing of a particular sketch the pupils can be invited to take the part of one character in the story and the sketch is then shown again in such a way that it is possible for the class to speak the role of that character.

The Heath de Rochemont *Parlons Français* course was originally produced on television in the United States to promote language teaching in elementary schools where a teacher qualified in French was rarely available. The intention was that the teacher would learn with the class and in follow-up lessons would simply lead the class in oral exercises based on the programme; he was not expected to add any new material at all. In Glasgow the same course has been used in a rather similar way on closed-circuit TV for the teaching of French in primary schools. The course itself is supplemented by videotaped scenes in which children from various schools in the city have participated in follow-up work based on the lessons of the course. In this way television is endeavouring to give the maximum amount of help to the teacher in providing not only a course complete in itself, but also an indication of how the course is being used, and with what degree of success, in other schools. It is interesting to compare this with the work of Telescuola in Italy in language teaching programmes. There a small representative group of pupils are brought to the studio for their lesson, so that the TV teacher can adjust his teaching to the performance of these sample children. The teachers in the schools can at the same time profit a great deal from watching the methods of the skilled teacher in the studio, who may have better opportunities of keeping abreast of recent developments in language teaching than the busy teacher in a remote school.

The *Parlons Français* course has been criticised for being too structural. Although the scenic décor is abundant, the characters varied and interesting, and the whole production very attractively presented, the basic method of teaching is constant repetition of structures rather than the exploiting of situation. Sometimes Anne Slack appears on the screen simply drilling the pupils in the repetition of structures for quite considerable periods of time. The distinctive potentiality of TV as a language teaching medium lies in the use that can be made of situation. This has been fully explained by Pit Corder,[1] and present developments in the use of TV for language teaching are largely concentrating on means of using the situational possibilities of the medium to the best advantage.[2] As many local education authorities are either setting up their own closed-circuit TV system or considering doing so soon, it may well be that language courses on TV may become increasingly common in all types of school in the next ten years or so. If and when it becomes as easy to record a TV broadcast on videotape as it is at present to record a sound programme, the use of language teaching TV programmes in schools will forge rapidly ahead.

[1] See S. Pit Corder, *English Language Teaching and Television,* Longmans, 1960, pp. 44-55. Also S. Pit Corder, *The Visual Element in Language Teaching,* Longmans, 1966.

[2] A wide survey of the use of TV in language teaching in Europe is given in R. Hickel, *Modern Language Teaching by Television,* Council for Cooperation of the Council of Europe, 1965.

We should also remember that the scope of language teaching by TV goes far beyond the schools, which are our immediate concern here. In some parts of South America where adequate numbers of teachers are not available, Spanish has been taught to large numbers of the indigenous peoples, mainly adults, who need Spanish to help them practically in raising the standard of their living. In Europe too TV language courses have been followed by large numbers of viewers in their homes. Such teaching could be a most important factor in the educational, social and economic development of a country.

General Assessment

We have been surveying a whole range of new techniques, new types of courses, new ways of going about language teaching. These new techniques derive largely from developments in linguistic and psychological research that have helped to illuminate the basic issues of what language is and how it is to be learned. At the same time these techniques make free use of every resource that technology can offer, whether it be tape-recorder, projector, radio or television, to apply the principles of language learning more efficiently. As a result of our survey our view of language teaching should be completely revitalised. We are developing a clearer purpose, a better understanding of what language learning really involves, and a much closer relationship between work in the classroom and the wider reality of spoken language in all human affairs.

The aspect of these new developments that has received most publicity of recent years is the language laboratory, which we shall examine more closely in the following chapter. A language laboratory is in itself only a set of valuable equipment that can be used in language teaching. It is neither a method, nor a course. To be used effectively it presupposes many of the developments that we have been considering in this chapter, but it is not itself essential to these new developments. The language laboratory is the exterior facility for developing in a concentrated way some, but not all, of the language learning activities that we have been considering.

What lies at the centre of the revitalised language teaching that is growing up is not just a whole set of technological gadgetry, but rather a method of teaching which uses the latest findings of linguistic and psychological research. We are not superimposing a few slick gimmicks on an old pattern. A completely new pattern of language teaching is arising—new in its objectives, new in its methods, new in its organisation. The salient features in the modern languages lesson will no longer be the textbook, the substitution exercise, the written translation and the written free composition. The emphasis is shifting to the recorded voice, the dialogue, oral pattern practice and oral composition.

Language teaching has got to become more efficient. We must obtain far better results in terms of pupils' performance in the language as a result of the language courses in our schools. The new techniques will be justified if they are more efficient than the traditional teaching of languages. We need not be afraid of efficiency, for what is more efficient is more human. To ask pupils to labour at endless written exercises in a strange language, to learn difficult grammatical rules unrelated to the reality of speech, or to toil at impossibly difficult translation work is, in a sense, inhuman. It is putting the pupils to a work of doubtful value and at the same time denying them satisfying experience in the use of a foreign language. On the other hand an audio-lingual course that teaches speech, with all its richness and its complexities, provides an experience that cannot fail to enrich the pupil's awareness of man's ability to communicate. Such a course is truly human. At the same time it can be every bit as demanding academically as a conventional course in language work. The discipline may be an oral one rather than a written one, but it is a discipline that stretches every pupil to the limits of his ability.

6

Language Laboratories

As early as the late 1940s rather primitive forms of language laboratories were being used in the United States. As magnetic recording facilities were developed and recording machines became less expensive, the use of such equipment for language teaching became more widespread. A national survey conducted in the U.S.A. in 1957 showed that in that year sixty-four public and private secondary schools, and 240 public and private institutions of higher education, were using laboratory facilities for foreign language instruction. The use of these facilities was given considerable impetus by the provisions of the National Defense Education Act of the following year. By 1961 it was estimated that about 2,500 secondary schools and about 700 colleges and universities had some kind of language laboratory. In the meantime E. M. Stack's authoritative work on language laboratory teaching had appeared.

American suppliers of language laboratory equipment, eager to expand their sales abroad, found about this time that the potential market in Britain was almost completely apathetic. It is claimed that the first language laboratory to operate in this country was installed by the Shell Petroleum Company, who used modified dictating machines, linked with an inter-communicating system to teach Indonesian to members of their staff. In 1961, however, Ealing Technical College was the first educational establishment in Britain to install and operate a full-scale language laboratory, which in this case was supplied by the Educational Foundation for Visual Aids and used Ferrograph tape-decks. This installation evoked enormous interest throughout the country and a constant stream of visitors came to Ealing to see the laboratory and the work being done there. It was particularly fortunate that what they saw was not simply a mechanical installation. Under the direction of Miss Mabel Sculthorp, who was then Head of the Department of General Studies at Ealing, the problems of language laboratory teaching were being seriously tackled. In particular audio-lingual courses in various languages were being developed and used in the language laboratory. The college ran a number of intensive language courses, mainly for business executives, and for this type of work at least, the staff became convinced that language laboratory facilities were a positive aid to speedy and thorough learning of a foreign language.

Colleges, universities and schools throughout the country began to realise the possibilities that this type of language teaching offered. At the same time audio-visual courses, especially *Tavor* and *Voix et Images de France,* were becoming more widely known, and the two developments were seen as related to one another. Various suppliers rapidly began to offer language laboratory equipment of varying quality and at varying prices. Towards the end of 1962 an enquiry showed that there were over forty installations in operation or firmly planned in various establishments throughout the country. Most of these were in technical colleges or colleges of commerce, but a thirty-two-booth laboratory was in use at Chorley Grammar School, and a few other schools had either just installed or were about to install laboratories of various sizes. From then on expansion has been rapid. In 1965 a survey showed that of 452 language laboratories in Britain, 190 were in secondary schools, 124 in technical colleges and other establishments of further education and twenty-nine in universities. About seventeen different suppliers are now competing in offering various types of equipment, some of which have been enormously improved as a result of practical experience. It is now estimated that there are more than 500 language laboratories in Britain.

What is a Language Laboratory?

A language laboratory is a teaching room equipped with electronic devices for recording or reproducing the human voice that are arranged in such a way as to be useful in language teaching. Within this broad definition there is a great deal of variety, but one can distinguish, generally speaking, two main types of laboratory, known as the *broadcast* type and the *library* type. In the first of these the student has no opportunity for recording his own voice, but, sitting at his own position, which may be a normal classroom desk, he hears a voice in his headset, to which he responds orally. He may or may not have a microphone to convey his response to the teacher's headset. In the library type of laboratory, which is now the usual type of installation, the student has in addition the possibility of recording his own responses and usually the possibility of working at his own speed independently of the rest of the class. This implies too that there is a certain measure of sound-proofing between the various student positions.

A typical installation of this kind would be housed in a room slightly larger than a normal classroom. The teacher's desk is in fact the console and has built into it all the electrical equipment that allows him to control the operation of the laboratory. Facing him are the students' semi-sound-proof booths, where the students sit, each with his own listening and recording facilities. At the console the teacher has a bank of switches and controls, by which he can put himself into communication with all or any of the students. He also has in the console the programme source or sources—that is, the tape-recorders or record-players on which the recordings of the programmes are played. From the programme source the programme can be put out to the students' booths and recorded on the master tracks of the students' tapes. There is usually a variety of programme sources so that, if so desired, two or more groups of students can work in the laboratory independently, but simultaneously. While the students are working on the programme that has been dubbed on to their tapes, the teacher at the console can monitor the work of each; that is to say, he can listen to what is being heard and said in each booth. At the turn of a switch he can interrupt any student to correct or help him in his work. Sitting at the console he can either stop the student's tape, or ask him to stop it, while he explains a point to the student through the intercom system of the laboratory. In this way he can give the student a little individual tuition before asking him to proceed with his work. Meanwhile the rest of the class continue to work, undisturbed by the intervention of the teacher's voice in one booth. If he wishes, the teacher can address the whole class through his microphone, or he can conduct a conversation with a group of students in which they can speak to him, he to them, and they to one another. The teacher can play the recorded responses of one student so that the whole class can hear them, if this is needed, or he can record at the console the efforts of any student, or of all in turn, a facility that is very useful for testing and marking oral work.

In each booth the student receives the programme from the console and records it on the master track of the tape in his machine. This operation is known as *dubbing* and may have been done before the student entered the laboratory, in which case he can start work at once independently of the console. The machine in each booth is a twin-track tape-recorder of which each track can operate independently. The programme from the console is recorded on track one, and usually this cannot in any way be erased by the student; it can only be erased by operating controls at the console or by putting the tape on a bulk-eraser. Track two is then available entirely for the student's responses. It is possible for him to listen to the programme recorded on track one and at the same time to record his responses to this programme on track two. In the programme itself instructions are given to the student about how he is to respond in any particular drill, and in any case he will have been instructed in this before coming to the laboratory.

The nature of the work done by the student in the booth can be of many various kinds. The teacher has complete liberty to devise whatever type of exercise he thinks appropriate. He could require the student to listen to a considerable piece of prose or dialogue, or even poetry, before giving any kind of response on the student track. There is certainly a place for such an exercise in linguistic study. But drills that involve short utterances to be repeated or changed or answered in some way by the student are much more common. Such drills seem to exploit the possibilities of the language laboratory very fully. While the teacher is free to devise what drills he will, we are going to describe here the operation of these drills which are now commonly used in language laboratories and which have been found to be effective.

After each utterance on the master track there is a pause on that track, during which the student makes his response, which is recorded at once on the student track. The correct response is then given on the master track so that the student knows at once whether he was right or wrong. A pause follows during which the student can if necessary repeat the correct response. Then the next item in the drill follows and the same procedure is repeated. The sequence on the tape for each item is therefore as follows:

Master track	Stimulus		Correct response	
Student track		Response		Corrected response

When the student has completed the drill he can wind his tape back to the point where he started and replay both tracks simultaneously. He will thus hear the responses he made and compare these with the voice on the master track which gives the correct form of the response. If he is not satisfied with his efforts he can return to the start of the drill and work it again. Automatically he will erase his previous recording, record his fresh responses and leave the master track untouched.

Typical of such a drill in French would be an exercise in which the student is asked to replace by pronouns the direct object noun in any given sentence. For example:

Master track: *Je ferme la porte.*

Student response: *Je la ferme.*

Then would follow the correct response on the master track

and the student could repeat this if necessary. Succeeding items in the same drill might be:

Master track: *Il mange le gâteau.*
Student response: *Il le mange.*
Master track: *Nous cherchons les enfants.*
Student response: *Nous les cherchons.*

The possibilities for teaching pronunciation, intonation, reading, as well as drilling the use of grammatical forms and structures, are many and varied. We shall examine some of the most usual drills in the next section.

Such a system of teaching offers clear advantages over the normal classroom situation. First, the recordings provide a faithful and untiring source of linguistic models given orally and, if desired, by a range of various voices. This relieves the teacher of the task of always providing the linguistic models of speech with his own voice, and frees him to some extent for the vital task of teaching. Second, the equipment offers the possibility for each student to work at his own speed on material suited to his own ability and achievement. If he can get no further than the first exercise he can stay on this for the whole of the lesson, while another student may go on to two or three other exercises. Third, each student is working, either listening or responding, for the whole of his time in the booth. In normal classroom conditions each student would have only a few minutes of any one lesson in which he could respond directly to the teacher's voice and be corrected by the teacher. Fourth, each student works in relative isolation and need not be inhibited by having to speak out in the hearing of a whole class. Fifth, the student can record his own voice, hear it replayed and make comparisons with the model on the master track. Finally, spoken language can be presented systematically in a carefully prepared progression and each structure can be thoroughly drilled.

The language laboratory has, however, its limitations. It does not provide for the teaching of meaning. When a drill is worked by a class it is assumed that the meanings of the sentences concerned are already known. These would normally be taught in classroom lessons arranged in conjunction with sessions in the laboratory. We would expect a class to spend only part of its language learning time in the laboratory, since there are other important activities to be undertaken in language learning besides those that can be done in the laboratory. Sometimes an audio-visual course is used in a laboratory and students watch a screen while they sit and listen in their booths. This provides context for the linguistic utterances and is a means of teaching meaning. But all the complexity of the laboratory is not necessary for audio-visual teaching, and it would probably be better to use the audio-visual course in a normal classroom before the class came into the laboratory. The students could then make the fullest use of the laboratory equipment when they are actually in the booths.

We should also remember that linguistic drilling in a laboratory is not real-life conversation. It has none of the unexpected turns, the sharp cut-and-thrust, the sudden interruptions, the unfinished sentences, the exclamations and other peculiarities of real dialogue. At the best it can only be a training in the skills of speech. These skills must be later used in real-life situations if they are to develop adequately. The language laboratory is an excellent training ground, but experience of reality must also be known by the student if that training is to be really effective.

Types of Laboratory Exercise

The language laboratory, as described in the previous section of this chapter, is a piece of educational equipment which the teacher has to use to the best advantage. His own imagination and ingenuity will devise various ways of making the best use of the equipment. In describing here various types of language laboratory exercise it is certainly not suggested that these are the only possible ones. The reader no doubt will think of others. These standard types of exercise have mostly been set out by Stack[1] in his important book, and other writers such as

[1] E. M. Stack, *The Language Laboratory and Modern Language Teaching*, Oxford University Press, 1960.

Hilton[1] and Turner[2] have largely repeated what Stack has said.

The simplest type of laboratory exercise is straightforward *repetition*. A word or sentence is given by the master track and the student has to repeat it. This exercise would be used mainly for teaching pronunciation and intonation, but would also have considerable value in introducing complex structures. When the exercise is extended to embrace a passage of prose, or possibly of poetry, it becomes a training in reading or a part of literary study. For this purpose it is best to record the passage read by a native speaker and then to *explode* the recording. This means that the passage is dubbed from one tape to another, and pauses left on the tape after each phrase or sentence. This procedure ensures that the intonation of each phrase is exactly what it would be if the unnatural pauses were not there. When using the exploded passage the pupil may be asked simply to repeat after the tape, or, at a later stage, with a printed version of the passage before him, he may be required to read each phrase in the pause before it occurs on the master track. Thus he has to anticipate the rendering of each phrase that was given by the original reader.

Analogy drills are those exercises that endeavour to make the student produce a sentence of similar structure but not identical to the one given on the master track. For example:

1. M. *Cette dame est charmante. Et ce monsieur?*
   S. *Ce monsieur est charmant.*
2. M. *Je vais à la piscine. Et Paul?*
   S. *Paul va à la piscine.*

A drill compiled on the model of the first example here would thoroughly teach the agreement of adjectives in certain types of sentence. The second example shows how a drill could be used to give thorough practice in the use of various parts of an irregular verb.

A very large number of exercises fall into the category of *mutation drills*. These, as the name suggests, are drills in which

[1] J. B. Hilton, *The Language Laboratory in School,* Methuen, 1964.
[2] J. D. Turner, *Introduction to the Language Laboratory,* University of London Press, 1965.

one part of the given sentence has to be changed in some way. A few examples, taken from various drills will give an idea of the possibilities:

3. Changing to the negative:
   M. *Je me lève à six heures.*
   S. *Je ne me lève pas à six heures.*
4. Changing to another tense:
   M. *Der Zug fährt nach Köln.*
   S. *Der Zug fuhr nach Köln.*
5. Placing an adverb in a sentence:
   M. *déjà. Il est parti.*
   S. *Il est déjà parti.*
6. Changing a structure:
   M. *Voilà un élève qui est riche.*
   S. *C'est un élève riche.*
   M. *Voilà un homme qui est beau.*
   S. *C'est un bel homme.*

In Chapter 3 we met structure drills of a kind that is sometimes called *open-ended*—that is, they can continue almost indefinitely. An example, this time from an exercise in teaching English, will make clear how these can be used:

7. M. *I have a book on the table.*
   S. *I have a book on the table.*
   M. *pen.*
   S. *I have a pen on the table.*
   M. *she.*
   S. *She has a pen on the table.*
   M. *in her hand.*
   S. *She has a pen in her hand.*
   M. *holds.*
   S. *She holds a pen in her hand.*
   M. *I.*
   S. *I hold a pen in my hand.*

It is very clear here that what is really being taught is the structure, as we saw in connection with pattern practice in Chapter 3.

Fixed-increment drills are exercises in which the same phrase or group of words has to be added to a sentence or part of a sentence. Sometimes changes will be required when the increment is added. Examples:

8. Adding *They say that . . .* to each sentence:
   M. *He is mad.*
   S. *They say that he is mad.*
   M. *They are very tired.*
   S. *They say that they are very tired.*
9. Prefixing each fragment with *Il faut que.*
   M. *Je vais en France.*
   S. *Il faut que j'aille en France.*
   M. *Nous apprenons l'espagnol.*
   S. *Il faut que nous apprenions l'espagnol.*

Here we can see that example 8 is of a much simpler kind than example 9, because no change in the form of the words is required when *They say that* is prefixed.

A rather difficult type of exercise is *paired-sentence drill,* where two sentences have to be joined together in a pre-arranged way. Examples:

10. M. *Dort steht ein Mann. Er ist alt.*
    S. *Dort steht ein alter Mann.*
11. M. *La ferme est à deux kilomètres d'ici. Vous parlez de la ferme.*
    S. *La ferme dont vous parlez est à deux kilomètres d'ici.*
12. M. *Faites attention! Ne cassez pas la vitre!*
    S. *Si vous aviez fait attention, vous n'auriez pas cassé la vitre.*

The exercise may consist of answering a question according to a set pattern. This could be simply to give a negative answer with a repetition of the statement in negative form. For example:

13. M. *Haben Sie einen roten Bleistift?*
    S. *Nein, ich habe keinen roten Bleistift.*
14. M. *Est-ce que votre frère est malade?*
    S. *Non, il n'est pas malade.*

Or it may be required in English to give short form answers in the positive. For example:

15. M. *Does Robert learn Latin?*
    S. *Yes, he does.*
    M. *Have you been to Canada?*
    S. *Yes, I have.*

All these examples require an answer in a definite form; there is only one right answer, and therefore the master track can provide the correct answer after the student has had time to respond. In this way reinforcement is given to the student's learning, and he is encouraged by knowing at once that he is right. If on the other hand he is wrong he has an opportunity of correcting himself at once. But we shall have a number of exercises that we wish to undertake which involve answers that may be different from each student and yet each student may be right. It is also possible to work such exercises in the laboratory, but the pattern will be a little different. We may have a comprehension exercise, in which a passage is first heard on the master track; the students listen to this twice and then hear a series of questions, which they have to answer one by one, about the subject matter of the passage. When they have recorded their answers the teacher can hand out the printed form of the passage and ask the students to replay. Following the printed version they will in most cases be able to see if their answers were correct or not. A study of a passage in this way can lead to work on literature. If the passage is taken from a work of literature the experience of hearing it read before the printed version is seen, can give fresh meaning to the passage by bringing out its full beauty and power in an oral rendering.

A Cycle of Lessons

The period in the language laboratory has a specific purpose. It is not the time for teaching meaning, as we have seen, nor is it the time for explaining new grammatical rules or forms. We must assume that every word and every structure used in a particular period in the laboratory is already well known to the class. The purpose of the drills, as far as grammar is concerned, is to give extensive practice in the use of certain structures and in manipulating them. This experience will help to deepen the knowledge that the students have of the grammar concerned, so that this knowledge sinks down in the mind to the subconscious level of skills and habits. In the same way, language laboratory exercises in pronunciation do not explain how certain sounds are made, but give extensive practice in the use of those sounds. The laboratory is a kind of workshop where apprentices gain experience in performing those skills that have been explained to them and demonstrated before them. It follows from this that not all the language teaching will take place in the laboratory, there must be normal classroom work as well. Indeed effective use of the laboratory is dependent on good teaching in the classroom beforehand, and will be improved if there are adequate follow-up lessons as well.

In any school the member of staff responsible for the administration of the language laboratory will need to decide how often each class is to have a lesson in the laboratory. In a typical three-stream grammar school where French is taught to all pupils from the first year and German to one or two groups from the third year, it will be found that there is not time in a thirty-five period week for each language class in the school to have more than one or two periods each week in the language laboratory, if every class is to have a fair share of the time available. At Chorley Grammar School it was found that those classes which could most profit from considerable time in the laboratory were the first forms and the weaker sets in the middle school. There the first-year classes were allocated three periods each per week in the laboratory out of five periods per week of French teaching.[1] At another school it was found that three periods per week in the laboratory was too much for one class. Probably we shall find that the most usual thing for a class to spend either one or two periods each week in the laboratory, and it may well be that one period out of four or five weekly lessons would be more suitable than two.

[1] Hilton, *op. cit.*, p. 115.

If this lesson were the third in a weekly cycle of five, we could start in the first lesson of the week with oral work related to a passage in the course-book, a dialogue, or oral material composed by the teacher around a certain topic. This work would involve the teaching of a certain amount of new vocabulary and at some point probably the explanation of items of new grammar arising in the passage or dialogue. In the second lesson this work would be revised, perhaps a brief dictation or other written exercise could be worked, and then in the final section of the lesson the drills that were going to be worked in the language laboratory the next day would be introduced to the class. The nature of each drill would be explained and several examples from each drill would be worked orally with the class, the pupils responding in chorus to the stimulus from the teacher. At the same time the teacher would have to ensure that all the vocabulary used in the drills was thoroughly known, and that the class was acquainted with the grammar underlying the drills. Then would come the third lesson of the week in the laboratory. The class should be able to go straight into the booths and start work at once without any time being spent on initial explanation. During the lesson the teacher would need to make a note of any problems arising in the work, and an explanation of these would occupy the first part of the fourth lesson of the week. The next part of that lesson would then be occupied with oral work on the original passage or dialogue, in which the teacher would constantly bring out the structures that had been drilled the previous day in the laboratory. This should help to relate the drills worked in the laboratory more closely to real-life communication. Then the final period of the week would be available for revision, written work, work on a reader, or any other activity the teacher wished to make use of.

If two periods in the laboratory were desired in one week, it would probably be advisable for the first session to concentrate on repetitive exercises of pronunciation and intonation, and for the second session later in the week to be mainly devoted to structure drills. The weekly cycle of lessons could then be: (1) in the classroom, the initial oral study of new material in a passage or dialogue; (2) in the laboratory, pronunciation and reading exercises on this material; (3) in the classroom, grammatical explanation of structures in the passage or dialogue, and preparation for laboratory work; (4) in the laboratory, work on structure drills; (5) in the classroom, follow-up and consolidation of this by oral and written work. Such a plan is no more than a suggestion and various alternatives would be possible. For example, the second lesson of the cycle, instead of concentrating on pronunciation, could relate mainly to the aural comprehension of the passage studied the previous day, the pupils being expected to listen to it, understand it, and answer questions on it, without the printed version in front of them. The essential is that work in the laboratory should be closely related to the normal work in the classroom, and that there should be both preparation before the laboratory lesson and follow-up after it.

In cases where an audio-visual course is being used in conjunction with a language laboratory it would be necessary to dovetail the above cycle of lessons with the kind of scheme for audio-visual work that we were considering in the previous chapter. If possible the audio-visual presentation should take place in the classroom and work in the laboratory should follow later. At the laboratory stage the visual element would not be necessary, as meanings should be well known before the class enters the laboratory. The tape-recordings of the audio-visual course could be used in the laboratory without the visual element. However, a completely different method is possible. Showing the film-strip in the laboratory, the teacher could require the pupils to give from memory the utterance appropriate to each frame. This assumes, of course, that work in the classroom would have already made them very familiar with the material. Each pupil would give the utterance as well as he could recall it, and then the correct version could be played to each booth from the console.

We notice here how much variety is possible in using this sort of equipment. This necessitates that the teacher should plan his work carefully. Again, it cannot be stressed too much that we are not simply appending a few novel activities to the traditional routine of work. An entirely new pattern of teaching is emerging, and this involves a new pattern of lessons within each weekly cycle. The work in the language laboratory must take its place as an integrated part of that cycle, and we must plan accordingly.

Monitoring

When suitable drills have been prepared for any particular class, when the pupils have been initiated into the working of the laboratory, when the weekly cycle of lessons has been planned and started, when at last each pupil is seated in his booth, with headset on and spools turning reassuringly in front of him, the teacher will probably relax at the console with a deep inward sigh of relief. Is this where the machine takes over? The former headmaster of Chorley Grammar School has explained with entertaining humour how easy it is for a teacher to operate the equipment with apparent success and yet fail to exploit its real possibilities.[1] It is precisely at this point, when the pupils are at work in the booths, that the teacher is confronted with the task of learning what is for him an entirely new technique: he has to *monitor*.

Monitoring involves that by careful operation of his switches the teacher listens to the work of one pupil after another, passes comments here and there, ensures that all are working and helps certain ones to do better work. Monitoring can be done entirely from the console, even without seeing the pupil to whom one is talking. Alternatively it is possible on some types of equipment to walk around the booths with a headset on and plug in at any student position to give help on the spot. The console method is quicker, but there may be advantages at times in coming alongside the pupil in the booth. The main difficulty is one of numbers. Some teachers experienced in this work maintain that one teacher can monitor no more than about half a dozen students satisfactorily. When one has a full class of thirty-two pupils, there is clearly no more than a minute or so for each booth in the course of a lesson. This is a quite inadequate proportion of

[1] Hilton, *op. cit.*, Chapter 4.

time for each pupil, for in the space of one minute a teacher can hardly get down to the real problem of any one learner. There is clearly a good case here for half classes in the language laboratory, but this would make time-tabling difficulties even greater, and produce the further problem of what is to be done with the other half of the class. With a full class in the laboratory the teacher must decide on a system in his monitoring. Probably he will do best to start by a quick survey of the whole laboratory. Pressing each switch in turn for a few seconds he can ascertain that all are working adequately. This may take nearly ten minutes. Then he should decide to concentrate on a group of pupils, it may be five only, to whom he is going to give detailed help in that lesson. It will be another group in the next laboratory lesson. The five need not be in adjacent seats, and in the course of the lesson the teacher can quickly drop in on the work of other pupils, without waiting to give detailed assistance. All this helps to make each pupil feel that the teacher may have his eye, or rather his ear, on him at any time.

It must not be assumed because a pupil can play back his own faulty response and can also hear the correct response on the master track, that he will therefore be aware of all the differences between the two. His ear needs to be trained to listen carefully. He may be too easily satisfied. He may not realize that he has to imitate not only pronunciation of individual sounds, but also the rise and fall of the voice throughout the sentence. All these things the teacher has to consider in monitoring. Let us suppose the teacher is listening to the efforts of a particular pupil. If there is a slight error of pronunciation the teacher may be able to slip in a word of correction without stopping the pupil's work and without clashing with the voice on the master track. But such an interjection will be confusing to some pupils. For most errors it will be better to stop the pupil's work, to stop his tape, or ask him to stop it, and to explain the point. The teacher can make the pupil repeat that part of the drill by acting as the voice on the master track himself, while the pupil responds, without any movement of the tape. When the teacher is satisfied, he can then ask the pupil to work that part of the drill again, working with his tape in the normal way.

In all this work the teacher has a great advantage if he has complete control from the console of the operation of the pupil's tape. With some types of equipment it is possible for the teacher to override the pupil's controls and stop, rewind or restart the pupil's tape. With other makes of language laboratory the teacher may have to ask the pupil to stop his tape, to rewind it or to find a particular point where an error occurred. The teacher may be wasting a great deal of precious time while the pupil fumbles with his switches or replays a section of tape to find the needed point. The teacher could do this much more quickly himself. There is a sense in which the equipment may be a hindrance, a kind of obstacle between teacher and taught, and the teacher may well feel that he would like to dispense with it for a few moments, throw off his headset, call out the pupil and speak to him face to face. There is no reason why he should not do this at times, but let the teacher also realise that he must so learn the skills of controlling the machinery, that the machine becomes no kind of obstacle. The language laboratory is no more than a teaching aid, it should never be a hindrance. The educational activity of teaching is the human experience of the impact of mind upon mind, the influencing of the pupil's mind, the development of his knowledge, skills and sensitivity by contact with other minds. If this educational activity is to take place in the laboratory, through the channel of the machinery, then the equipment must be absolutely mastered by the teacher, and perform exactly what he wishes it to in order to aid his teaching.

Some Problems

The first problem that presents itself to the would-be language laboratory user (assuming his school or college or local authority has the wherewithall and the intention to purchase a laboratory), is to decide which of the various makes now on the market is the most suitable for his purposes. It is not intended here to discuss the various makes. Developments and improvements take place so rapidly that makers tend to leap-frog one another in introducing improvements to their equipment. Some makers are endeavouring to provide superb equipment without much consideration of cost, others seek to produce equipment of minimum standard as cheaply as is reasonably possible. Most makers are working somewhere between these two extremes. It is essential, before purchasing, to examine the full range of equipment available. Teachers and local authorities should never be satisfied with one demonstration, but should always see an installation working, and talk to teachers who use it, before making a purchase of that type of equipment. It should also be noticed that not one type of equipment can be said to be best for all circumstances. According to the age of the pupils, the type of work undertaken, the nature of the school or college, the size of classes and other factors, so one type of laboratory or another may be most appropriate. Purchasers need to think out what they really require. Not all the extra facilities provided by some suppliers are as necessary as they might appear. Provision for the central matter of language learning is the essential requirement. If all this is clearly thought out, and the range of equipment considered, it should soon become apparent which type is the right one for purchase.

Teachers using language laboratories find that far from saving time the laboratory equipment involves a great increase in the amount of time and effort that they have to spend on their work. One of the reasons for this is the need to prepare materials. There may be as much as three or four hours' work involved in producing the recorded material for fifteen minutes' work in the laboratory. The teacher who is fully engaged on teaching duties in a school will not normally be able to find time to produce his own materials. Of course, schools will gradually build up a store of materials on tape, including structure drills, pronunciation and comprehension exercises, dialogues, literary passages and so on, using various native or non-native voices that may be available from time to time. Nevertheless, any school that has just installed a laboratory would do well to release one member of staff from about half of his teaching duties, for a term or a year, to enable him to produce some of this material. There is of course a good deal available commercially, but in many cases it will not be fully suitable. There are the *A-L M* courses, which are suitable for language laboratory use, but which advance rather too rapidly for junior forms in British grammar schools. There is the recorded material of various audio-visual courses such as *Voix et Images de France* or *Let's Speak French,* but these do not provide all the exercises that may be required, especially structure drills. There are *C.L.T. Basic Tapes*[1] which provide structure drills for laboratory use, but do not provide dialogues or passages for comprehension. Various conversation courses and some other materials are also available from the Tutor Tape Company.[2] But in all these commercially produced recordings the teacher is not likely to find a full language laboratory course that exactly fits his requirements. If he is able to purchase a good selection of this material, he will be very fortunate, and will be able to choose here and there what most suits his needs. But he will constantly find that vocabulary does not correspond with the course he is following in his school, and yet, as we have seen, it is vital that pupils should not meet unfamiliar words in the laboratory. A book such as Adam's *Language Laboratory Pattern Drills in French*[3] may be very useful in providing the teacher with an outline of various drills, which he can then record himself, adapting the vocabulary to the needs and knowledge of his own classes.

There is an increasing need nationally for linguistic materials on tape suitable for use in secondary school language laboratories. The ease with which one copy of a recorded course can be dubbed on to other tapes has meant that producers now recognise that this is bound to take place and include within the price of the tape the right to make copies for use within the same educational establishment. This of course keeps sales down and prices up, and therefore the

[1] *C.L.T. Basic Tapes,* supplied by Monitor Language Laboratories, Scrivener—SLT Ltd., 43-45 Queen's Road, Bristol 8.

[2] The Tutor Tape Company Ltd., 2 Replingham Road, London S.W.18.

[3] J. B. Adam, *Language Laboratory Pattern Drills in French; basic series,* Pitman, 1964.

production of a course on tape is a risky undertaking for a publishing firm, unless textbooks are also sold as an essential accompaniment to the tapes. The Nuffield Foundation's courses will go a long way towards meeting the needs of teaching in the eleven to thirteen age range, especially in Spanish, German and Russian. The continuation of this work will be under the auspices of the Schools Council, which has a subcommittee on modern languages. The National Committee for Research and Development in Modern Languages will no doubt consider this question and may produce some answers. There will need to be cooperation between the various parties concerned. The publishers may be willing to contribute their experience and knowledge of the publishing world, while some of the financial provision may have to come from the Department of Education and Science or from independent bodies, such as the Nuffield Foundation. The production of audio-lingual courses is an undertaking that involves team work at various levels; teachers, linguists, artists and technicians need to work together in devising the course, and publishers and other educational bodies need to cooperate in promoting the undertaking and in making such courses generally available to schools.

A further group of difficulties and problems concern administration within the school. There is first the question of timetabling which we have already considered, and which is closely linked with methods and policy of language teaching in the school. This is connected with the difficulty of the size of classes and whether it can be arranged to split classes into smaller groups for laboratory work. There is also the practical problem of breakdowns and servicing the equipment. A steward or technician, even if he is available only on a part-time basis, can give most valuable help, but experience seems to show that this is not essential. What is vital is that there should be an arrangement with the supplier or with some other firm, whereby any fault in the equipment can be repaired in the shortest possible time. Provision will also need to be made for classification and storage of tapes, for library listening facilities at certain times for some pupils, and for the use by the staff of the recording and editing room that should accompany

any laboratory. For all these administrative matters it is necessary that one member of staff, not necessarily the Head of the Modern Languages Department, should have the main responsibility for the laboratory, and should be deputed to do the organizational work involved.

The Real Value of a Laboratory

So much publicity has been enjoyed by language laboratories that it may be a little difficult to see their role in sober perspective. We have already seen that they have clear limitations. There are imporant tracts of language teaching that they cannot and do not provide for. They also produce a number of problems for the language teacher and it is doubtful whether they automatically solve any. The installation of a language laboratory in a school is certainly no panacea for all language teaching ills. It is rather a serious challenge to the languages staff, who will need to provide a great amount of hard work, perseverance and fortitude, will need to adapt themselves and their teaching to new ways and new ideas, and yet will have to retain the essential elements of their teaching, and themselves be masters of the machine.

Language laboratories have probably been most successful in crash courses for small groups of highly motivated adults, for example businessmen who need a language for their work. To persist week after week, month after month with the hard task of learning a language needs a good deal of motivation and determination. Work in the language laboratory can become boring, as structure after structure is drilled and the tape goes on relentlessly. One may even reach a point where one is repeating mechanically, perhaps correctly, but the words are passing through one's headset, and through one's head, without any real learning taking place. These are some of the dangers of which the teacher must be aware. But there is no doubt that in secondary schools, as well as in technical colleges, in colleges of education and in universities, language laboratories have a real contribution to make. Where languages are taught as a living means of communication, the laboratory can provide that systematic practice in the structures of the language that is so needful for a really competent grasp of the skill of speech in the foreign medium.

As the new pattern of language teaching becomes more clearly established it will probably become normal for grammar and comprehensive schools to have a language laboratory, and maybe for some of the surviving secondary modern schools too. We shall have to regard the laboratory no longer as a strange phenomenon, nor as a new-comer, nor as a luxury; it will become part and parcel of the language teaching system. We have no need to fear the machine. Here is a wonderful tool that the skilful teacher can use to give deeper understanding to his pupils of the true nature of language skills.

7

Examinations

When curriculum changes come about in education, whether these concern the method of teaching or the subject matter taught, it is clear that changes will also be necessary in the examinations that evaluate this education. This is particularly true of the developments in modern language teaching that we have considered in the last two chapters. Indeed developments in examining are not only a result of changes in the curriculum, they also have a feedback effect which influences the curriculum. So it has been that teachers have often pointed out that any large-scale change in the direction of new techniques is hindered by the examinations as they at present exist. While G.C.E. Ordinary level language papers remain largely a test of ability to use the written language, and a test by translation, teachers will naturally enough teach the written language and teach translation. This does not mean that teachers are satisfied with this situation. Indeed, quite apart from the development of audio-visual courses and language laboratories, there has for many years been a movement among languages teachers for the reform of examinations. This is why we include a consideration of examinations here in Part Two as part of our account of current developments. Radical changes in our national pattern of language teaching will take form only when public examinations also change the nature of the imprint they impose.

Ordinary Level

For many pupils in British secondary schools the main objective of their work in French or German is to secure a pass in one or both of these subjects in the G.C.E. examination at Ordinary level. For their teachers, too, an important objective is to get as many pupils through the examination as possible. In some cases the pupil's prospects of pursuing a university career or of entering the profession of his choice may depend on a pass at Ordinary level in a foreign language. As examination subjects, modern languages enjoy some prestige, and it is commonly thought, though the idea may not be fully justified, that a pass in French is worth more to the candidate as a proof of intellectual ability, than a pass in what might be called a more practical subject. It is not surprising that the fourth and fifth years of the grammar school course are directed very largely at success in the Ordinary level examination.

Although the examination is conducted by some ten different boards, operating almost independently, there is a remarkable sameness about the form the examination takes as set by each board. There is always a test involving translation from the language into English, and usually there are two different passages to be translated. Until recently there has always been a test involving translation from English into the language. From 1964 onwards the Associated Examining Board has abandoned this test, and four other boards are now planning to introduce alternative syllabuses without prose translation into the language. There is always a composition or essay question in the examination in some form, though in some cases this involves the reproduction of a story read aloud to the candidates. Most boards also include some kind of comprehension question in which the candidates have to write, either in English or in the language, answers to questions on a passage printed on their question papers. These are the four types of written test that usually occur, though the writing of the composition may, as we have said, be combined with an aural comprehension element. There are also three types of test involving the spoken language. All boards include a dictation in the examination, and this of course is a test of written accuracy as well as of aural ability. A few boards set a test of aural comprehension in which the candidates have to answer questions on a passage read aloud to them. Finally, all boards include an oral test, which is usually conducted by a visiting examiner, and which can usually be divided into a reading test and a conversation test. The Associated Examining Board allocates a quarter of the total number of possible marks to this oral test, but in some cases the maximum number of marks obtainable for the oral test is no more than 10 per cent of the total for the whole examination in the subject. There is some considerable variation among the boards in the relative weighting of marks for the various tests, but generally speaking by far the largest proportion of marks is awarded for the tests in translation from and into the language and for the composition tests.

Criticisms of Ordinary Level

The first and most common criticism of Ordinary level is that oral aspects of the language and aural-oral skills are badly neglected. If our main purpose is to teach the pupils to understand the spoken language and to speak it, then this is certainly true. Even the 25 per cent. of the total marks allocated by the A.E.B. to the oral test is quite inadequate if we view this aspect of language work as more important than writing skills. Secondly, the use of translation from English into the foreign language is criticised on the grounds that translation into a foreign language is a difficult exercise inappropriate to this stage of language learning. Translation is an art quite distinct from the ability to use a language. It presupposes the knowledge of one language in addition to the mother tongue, but it is additional to this and is not a valid test of ability to use the language productively. It may also encourage the wrong habits of mind. Thirdly, a very large proportion of the marks, sometimes more than 50 per cent of them, are to be had for writing in English in the examination room. Translation and comprehension tests have to be written in English. Examiners' reports frequently complain that candidates have lost marks heavily on account of poor English or poor English spelling. It does not speak well for the validity of the examination if candidates can pass or fail a test in a foreign language on the score of their ability in English. Finally, the examination requires a certain precision of thought and an accuracy in dealing with detail which, while it has something to do with language, is not language itself. It is not meant here to advocate inaccuracy of grammar or to neglect precision in matters vital to the language itself. But marks are often lost for failing to put an *and* for every *et,* for translating *ce* by the English definite article, whereas these details are of minor importance compared with the essential need to grasp the meaning of the sentence as a whole. Professional and literary translators are not tied to a slavish reproduction of details of this kind. In the interests of reliability the examiners have been compelled to require something as near to word-for-word transliteration as the languages involved will allow.

In the light of changes in the aims and methods of language teaching that are now coming about it has become clear that what is needed is not a piecemeal adjustment of the examination, but a vital rethinking of the whole undertaking. We need to decide first of all what it is we wish to test. Having defined clearly what knowledge and what skills we are endeavouring to test, we must then proceed to devise reliable tests that do in fact measure this knowledge and these skills and nothing else. The Ordinary level examination as it now stands has been inherited from the past. An examination that may possibly have been appropriate for a certain type of pupil in our grammar schools some fifty or sixty years ago has been handed down to us, with some modifications, and is now applied in circumstances to which it is not suited. Historical reasons for the form of so vital a test are insufficient; we must have an examination that tests what we are teaching, adapted to the aims and methods of the very best teaching today.

The first question is: What do we wish to test? It is not difficult to define the body of knowledge to be tested. In the case of French the lexical extent of the linguistic knowledge required would probably be something like *Le Français Fondamental, deuxième degré.* The grammatical knowledge required could equally well be defined, and a number of grammar books, written specifically for examination classes, contain a statement of the grammar usually required.[1] A similar body of linguistic items could be defined for German, Russian, Spanish or any other language. But we are not only testing knowledge, we are testing skills. The four basic language skills are (1) aural comprehension (2) oral expression, (3) comprehension of the written word, (4) expression in writing. These skills are combined in various ways in different language activities; for example (3) and (2) are combined in reading aloud, (1) and (4) are combined in dictation, (1) and (2) are combined in conversation. But not all aspects of these skills are used in any one activity. Reading aloud is not a full test of oral expression because it does not involve the mental formation of new sentences; dictation may involve only a partial comprehension aurally and is not a full test of all aspects of written expression. In any case we shall need to decide what relative importance is to be attached to each of these four skills. Are they all to have equal importance and each carry 25 per cent of the marks? Or are the first two more important than the others? These questions are to some extent decided for us by the types of tests that can be and have been devised. If a particularly reliable type of test exists, we shall find a strong reason for using it. Conversely, we cannot expect an examination to be highly esteemed if the tests it most prominently uses are known to be of doubtful reliability.

In any examination that is intended to replace the present Ordinary level, we would expect at least half of the marks to be awarded for aural-oral skills and for knowledge of the language evidenced by the use of these skills. In assessing skills and knowledge that relate to the written language, we would expect considerable emphasis to be laid on original expression in the language in writing. Translation, as such, is not an activity that we should test at this stage, though it could possibly be used as a test of comprehension of the written word. These are only most general statements about what we are

[1] e.g. W. F. H. Whitmarsh, *Simpler French Course for First Examinations*, Longmans, Section VI.

testing, and they leave many questions unanswered. For example, in testing oral expression we should have to decide how much relative importance to attach to pronunciation, intonation, fluency, extent of vocabulary, construction of sentences, and so on. In any case it is often difficult to divide language activities into departments, and we need to have an eye for the total language performance of the individual. Ultimately, the person who knows the language best is the person who can communicate most effectively in the foreign language situation when he is dependent on his ability in the language alone.

Types of tests to be used have been examined very thoroughly by Lado in his book, *Language Testing*[1]. But many of his tests are directed at testing such small sections of language knowledge that a truly vast quantity of tests would be required to accomplish what the Ordinary level examination sets out to do. Practical considerations of time and marking demand that more than one skill and a wide range of knowledge should be tested in one and the same test. However, any new form of the examination is bound to involve new types of tests and new methods of testing. Here it is noteworthy that the tape-recorder can now be used extensively to assist the examiner. Recorded versions of passages to be used for aural comprehension can be sent to the examining centres. Each candidate, wherever he is, will then hear the same voice in the test. Pupils will also be compelled to become accustomed to voices other than that of their teacher. In the second place recordings of the candidates' oral performance in a test can be sent to the examiner and scrutinised by him in some detail. Although the replaying of these recorded performances takes up a good deal of the examiner's time, there is a saving on travelling for examiners and greater possibilities of coordinating standards of oral examining. However, oral examining by tape-recording has its limitations. Examiners in oral English have found assessment by tape-recording unsatisfactory[2]; we should not

[1] R. Lado, *Language Testing*, Longmans, 1961.

[2] See a letter by A. Wise to *The Times Educational Supplement* of 20 September 1963, under the title 'Oral English'.

imagine that this method of examining has solved all our problems.

The M.L.A. Examination Project

In April 1963 the Modern Languages Association established a project which had as its objective to prepare an alternative Ordinary level syllabus in modern languages. Mr H. S. Otter, who was appointed director of the Project, started to work on the production of a syllabus that would exclude translation into the foreign language and increase the importance of oral communication. It was required that this new examination should be an alternative of a strictly comparable standard, that it should require only a similar amount of examining time to that needed in the current examination, and that it should be manageable in terms of large-scale administration.

Mr Otter prepared various aural-oral tests, involving the use of the tape-recorder, which were tried out in a group of Yorkshire schools in November 1963. This initial experiment was called Project I, and was no more than preparatory experience for the conduct of Project II, which was to be a full-scale examination covering a wide range of schools. This Project II was conducted in March 1964 and involved forty-five schools, most of them being in Yorkshire or in the West of England, but some as far afield as Wilhelmshaven and the Isle of Skye. Approximately 600 candidates were entered for French and 500 for German, drawn from A, B and C streams. In practically all cases the candidates were being entered for the normal G.C.E. Ordinary level examination with one of the examining boards the same year. Schools undertook to work the examination of the M.L.A. Project on a purely voluntary basis. After a full statistical analysis had been made of the results of this examination, Project III was organised. This was another full-scale examination conducted along similar lines to Project II, but with modifications introduced as a result of the experience gained. This examination was conducted in March 1965 and involved 650 candidates for French and 347 for German drawn from thirty-nine schools in widely different areas. A final report, giving a full account of the work and the statistical analyses of the results, was issued a year later.[1] In this report suggestions were put forward for an alternative syllabus, based on what had been done in Project III.

The various tests used in these experimental examinations were designed to test the candidate's ability to understand and use the spoken language as well as his ability to express himself in writing. Extensive use was made of tape-recordings. Recorded passages were sent to the schools, to be played to the candidates in aural comprehension tests. The reading and conversation tests were all conducted in the schools by the teachers and recorded on tapes which were then sent to the examiners for marking. One reading test was designed to test the candidate's ability to read correctly certain short phrases in which some specific item of pronunciation or intonation was being tested. In another reading test the candidate was required to read a prepared passage. In one conversation test the candidate was asked ten to fifteen questions chosen at random from a syllabus list of a hundred questions that had been issued before the examination; in another test the candidate was required to talk with the teacher on topics chosen at random by the teacher from a syllabus list.

In Project III multiple-choice tests were introduced. There was an aural comprehension test based on texts recorded by native speakers. The recorded texts and questions were spoken once only and candidates had to select the appropriate answer or comment from four printed responses in the language. Part of the reading comprehension test was also a multiple-choice test entirely in the language, based on passages of varying length, subject matter and style, each of which was followed by two or more questions. The use of these multiple-choice tests was an interesting experiment which produced very satisfactory results. Being objective tests, they produced particularly reliable scores.

In Project II only 35 per cent of the marks were awarded

[1] The Modern Language Association Examinations Project, *Report* 1963-1966. Issued at the Leeds University Institute of Education in March, 1966. Information about the M.L.A. Examinations Project is also contained in three articles by H. S. Otter that appeared in *Modern Languages*, Vol. XLVI, No. 1, March 1965, pp. 12-17; Vol. XLVI, No. 2, June 1965, pp. 57-9; Vol. XLVI, No. 4, December 1965, pp. 155-9.

for activities which did not essentially involve some aspect of the spoken language. Another 35 per cent of the marks were awarded for activities that did not involve any writing. The remaining 30 per cent of the marks were for activities that linked aural comprehension and writing. In Project III the weighting of marks was, if anything, rather more in favour of the skills of aural comprehension and speech. Dictation was not included in the examination; this rather sophisticated test can be a stimulating exercise but offers little that can not be dealt with by other tests.

The statistical analyses proved that in practically all the tests the distribution of marks was very satisfactory. There was also found to be a satisfactorily close correlation between the examination results and the schools' estimates. A comparison between results on Project III and the candidates' actual scores in the normal Ordinary level examination, taken later the same year, showed that Project III was not a type of examination that would produce wildly different results from the traditional papers, but its tests involved different activities with emphasis on the spoken language and its use. The M.L.A. Project as a whole has demonstrated that reliable marking of oral tests is possible, and that a large-scale examination in a foreign language that makes extensive use of recording techniques for oral tests can give dependable marks. In addition considerable experience has been gained in the conduct of such an examination both by the examiners and by the schools concerned.

Discussions took place from time to time between the Director of the M.L.A. Project and the various examining boards. Several of these have now put forward alternative syllabuses that do not include translation into the foreign language. The Joint Matriculation Board operated in 1966 an experimental syllabus based on the work of the M.L.A. Project, which included specially prepared multiple-choice tests of listening and reading comprehension, and which involved the recording of oral tests. It is possible that within a few years a number of examining boards may be conducting alternative Ordinary level examinations in modern languages along the lines developed by the M.L.A. Project.

The C.S.E. Examinations

In the years immediately following the Second World War the secondary modern schools rejoiced, or were supposed to be rejoicing, in the fact that their work was untrammelled by public examinations. As time went on, however, they began to yearn for the status and the prestige that an assessment of their work by public examination would give to them and their pupils. Increasing numbers of secondary modern schools entered a few of their pupils for G.C.E. Ordinary level papers, while examinations conducted by the Royal Society of Arts were frequently used for other pupils. The Beloe report[1] recommended an examination suitable for pupils who could not be expected to attain the standard of the G.C.E., and yet who might well profit from the incentive of an examination suited to their abilities. From the recommendations of this report the Certificate of Secondary Education arose. It is a regionally administered examination, which is controlled at every point by practising teachers who themselves act as examiners. It is intended for children of average ability—that is, the numerous pupils who stand in the middle or above the middle of the ability range in their age group, but who do not quite attain to the 20 per cent or so who attempt G.C.E. Ordinary level in four or more subjects.

The examination, which took place for the first time in the summer of 1965, can be taken in one of three ways. The most usual of these is Mode 1, according to which an external examination is set on a syllabus prepared by the relevant subject panel. Under Mode 2, a school or group of schools design their own syllabus, which is then examined externally. Mode 3 provides for the possibility of a school designing its own syllabus, and examining on it internally, while the examination is moderated externally. There are fourteen regional boards who are responsible for the administration of the examination in their areas. These boards award certificates to about 90 per cent of the candidates. The certificates are

[1] *Secondary School Examinations Other than the G.C.E.*, report of a committee appointed by the Secondary School Examinations Council in July 1958 (Beloe report), O.H.M.S., 1960.

graded at five levels, and grade one is said to be equivalent to a pass at G.C.E. Ordinary level.

The subject panels of the regional boards are composed of teachers, and therefore the syllabuses reflect what teachers themselves wish their pupils to be examined in. The most striking feature of the syllabuses and papers in modern languages which have been prepared by various boards, is the great importance that is everywhere attached to oral work. In most cases the proportion of marks allocated by the boards is something like 50 per cent for oral work and 50 per cent for written work. It is clearly the wish of teachers in the schools concerned that this should be so, and it is clearly their opinion that the approach to language learning that this involves is the right one for pupils of average ability.

A subcommittee of the Modern Language Association[1] has investigated the syllabuses of various boards and found that, although there is a good deal of variation in detail among the different boards, there is nevertheless a general pattern, which with modifications all boards seem to have adopted. The oral part of the examination usually consists of conversation and reading tests, dictation and an aural comprehension test. This latter usually requires that the candidates should answer in English questions given in English about a passage read to them in the language. In some cases these four tests together carry more than 50 per cent of the marks. In the written part of the examination no board sets translation from English into the foreign language, though some make use of translation into English. Reading comprehension tests are included in all cases, the questions sometimes to be answered in English and sometimes in the language. These tests are designed to assess the candidates' ability to read and understand a passage in the language. Free composition is also generally included in the written paper and may carry as much as 25 per cent of the total number of possible marks. The form of the composition test varies a good deal. Some boards also test background knowledge about the country or people concerned, or take into

[1] See P. C. Whitmore, 'C.S.E. Examinations in Modern Languages', in *Modern Languages*, Vol. XLVI, No. 1, March 1965, pp. 17-23.

consideration course work done by the pupils before the actual examination.

It is most interesting and encouraging to find how much importance teachers wish to place on aural-oral skills and on free expression in the language. It is most significant too that these skills are thought to be appropriate to pupils who are not in the upper quartile of the ability range. On the other hand there is something rather conventional about the type of test employed. While the emphasis on oral work may be quite different from the weighting of marks in Ordinary level papers, yet the type of test used by the boards so far is very reminiscent of G.C.E.

The Manchester School of Education has conducted a C.S.E. Research Project, which has been concerned with modern languages among other subjects. The interim report issued by the modern languages panel in March 1965 showed that the teachers and lecturers who composed this panel had decided to give 60 per cent of the marks in their experimental tests for achievement in aural-oral aspects of the work and 40 per cent only for written work. Many of the main conclusions of this Project are similar to those of the M.L.A. Project. Multiple-choice objective tests were used for testing knowledge of vocaublary, comprehension and knowledge about the country. Class teachers conducted the oral tests and recordings on tape were used for comprehension tests. Broadly speaking the form of examination arrived at was in three parts, which were the objective tests, two exercises in written expression one of which was made to result from the oral conversation test, and thirdly the oral expression and conversation tests. These included dictation and tests of oral composition, aural comprehension and reading.

An examination along these lines, which makes extensive use of objective testing, seems to have broken away from the traditions of G.C.E. and is more likely to provide the type of test most suited to C.S.E. candidates. It is to be hoped that the work of the Manchester Project will have considerable influence on the regional boards. Even without any further action by the boards themselves, there is the possibility, under

Mode 3, of teachers proposing examinations which are similar to the Manchester proposals. Perhaps the most encouraging feature of C.S.E. is that machinery has been set up for designing and operating a new type of examination that has built into it the possibility of being receptive to new ideas and enterprising schemes that teachers or research workers may develop.

Language Testing in Commerce

In a different sector of the education system parallel developments in language testing have been taking place. The growth of interest in the study of languages for use in commerce and business has been such that a group of industrial undertakings approached the Birmingham Chamber of Commerce with the object of developing practical examinations at various stages for testing businessmen and women who are languages students. In conjunction with the London Chamber of Commerce, the Birmingham Chamber produced a scheme of tests at any of three levels, and these first came into operation in January 1964. At the Elementary Grade the examination is an oral test lasting twenty minutes. Candidates are expected to be capable of two-way communication in the foreign language on simple everyday topics. Candidates for the Intermediate Grade are required to take an oral test lasting thirty to thirty-five minutes during which they must show that they have the conversational ability to get about in the foreign country without difficulty and sufficient confidence in the language to take their place socially. The subject matter of passages and recorded conversations used at this level is non-technical, but considerable powers of aural comprehension and oral expression are expected. At the Advanced Grade candidates are expected to be able to conduct the normal business of their company in the foreign language. The examination, which lasts fifty minutes, includes short tests in the written translation of passages read to the candidate or played from a recording. The candidate is also asked to talk about and discuss his job with the examiner who, in the course of the examination, speaks at the speed and in the manner of normal conversation.

It is interesting to notice that a need has been felt in commerce for examinations of this kind, and that an effort has been made to establish standards for the testing of oral proficiency. While these examinations are outside the range of normal language teaching in schools, we must remember that some pupils will go on to work that may involve ability in using a foreign language in commerce and may take similar tests.

The Influence of Examinations

There can be no doubt whatever that the form of an examination has a very appreciable influence on both the content and the method of teaching. Just as the G.C.E. examination has had a powerful influence on preserving a grammar–translation approach to language teaching in the middle forms of grammar schools, so the emphasis placed on oral work in the C.S.E. examination will be a determining factor in teaching methods in modern and comprehensive schools. The C.S.E. examination will extend its influence to the academic streams of the comprehensive schools and probably to the grammar schools too. If the new form of Ordinary level, developed by the M.L.A. Project, is accepted by the boards, this too will exert its influence. So long as the new type of examination remains an alternative, alongside the traditional type, this influence will be severely limited. Such a transitional period will be necessary. Eventually, however, radical changes may come in all possible types of Ordinary level papers, so that schools are obliged to adopt a reformed type of examination.

As we have already seen there are other very powerful developments at work in the schools and changes in approach to teaching are in no sense dependent on changes in terminal examinations. For many teachers the reformed type of G.C.E. will be a long overdue adjustment that brings the examination much more into line with their own ideas and teaching methods. It is new developments in method and new ideas of teaching that have themselves brought about the changes in examinations. A process of interaction between teaching and examining seems to be essential to the healthy functioning of the educational system. New methods of teaching must not be hampered by examinations, and new types of examinations must be tried out and proved reliable by experience. Provision for these vital developments to take place has been made in the way that the C.S.E. examinations have been set up. If we wish examinations to be the servants of true education, and not its masters, then continual adaptation and development must also take place in the G.C.E. examinations. The work of the M.L.A. Project and of the Manchester Research Project has in itself been excellent, but this work will need to be continued, developed and refined by the boards themselves.

The new examinations that are arising form part of the new pattern of language teaching. Courses that involve the use of audio-visual techniques or of language laboratories lead to new types of terminal tests. These in turn will open up the way for new prospects in post-Ordinary level courses. Professor Cruikshank has suggested an Advanced level course that would involve 'Précis-writing on the basis of listening to recorded speeches or conversations in the foreign language, and . . . much more free composition'.[1] Such activities would alternate with translation work. Oral work in the sixth form could be made much more demanding, and new techniques of examining at Advanced level would encourage this. As Professor Cruikshank also suggests, the texts studied need not be purely literary, but could be of a more historical or reflective nature, dealing in a general way with biography, current affairs, economics or politics.

The Joint Council of Language Associations has actively considered an alternative form of the Advanced level examination, that would give more prominence to linguistic as opposed to literary studies, and would also encourage a wider study of the foreign background as a whole.[2] Such an examination would be an alternative to stand alongside the existing Advanced level, but enjoying equal status. It has been

[1] J. Cruikshank, 'Alternatives to Literary Studies in Post "O" Level Language Courses', in *Modern Languages*, Vol. xlv, No. 1, March, 1964, pp. 18-20.

[2] See *Audio-Visual Language Journal*, Vol. 3, No. 2, Autumn, 1965, pp. 103, 104.

suggested that there should be an intensive aural-oral examination and three written papers—translation from and into the language, and free composition. The study of 'set books' would be replaced by the study of political and social history, geography, current political, social and economic affairs, and the arts, including literature. The four parts of the examination might each carry a quarter of the marks. The intention is not to remove literary studies from sixth-form modern languages courses, but rather to provide an alternative type of course, which would be more suited to the interests and needs of certain pupils. Such a course would lead either directly to posts in business and commerce, or to some of the new university courses that we shall consider later.

Part Three

The New Pattern

8

Foreign Language Teaching in Primary Schools

In Part Two we reviewed various current developments in language teaching techniques and in examining language skills. We are now going on to consider the impact of these developments at the three successive levels of primary, secondary and further education. At the same time we need to remember the influence of the trends of thought about language teaching which we outlined in Part One. These too contribute to what is actually taking place in schools and colleges. When we come, in this final Part of the book, to consider the practical outcome of these various trends and developments, we shall need to see how changes in language teaching are related to wider changes in the whole educational scene. Curriculum development in one group of related subjects—modern languages—cannot be divorced from what is happening elsewhere in our education. If we try to view these developments in a true perspective and in right relation to changes in other aspects of education, we shall see that a new pattern of language teaching is emerging in our educational system. This new pattern involves new methods of teaching, new emphases in the subject-matter, new types of courses, and also the fact that different types of pupils are following these courses and different types of teachers are giving them.

An Earlier Start

One of the clearest features of the new pattern is that a foreign language is being taught at a much earlier age than has been usual. It came to be accepted in the interwar years that eleven was on the whole the best age at which to begin language learning. No serious attempts were made to introduce language teaching into primary schools. In *Modern Languages*,[1] the Ministry pamphlet which appeared in 1956, a reference was made to the possibility of teaching a foreign language in primary schools, but the idea was not seriously entertained as a practice likely to become general. It was not until the early 1960s that significant developments began to take place. Up to that time, modern languages had been considered a truly grammar school discipline.

Yet it was generally believed, and explicitly stated in the Leathes report of 1918, that young children had a particular facility for acquiring spoken language. All the evidence available seems to confirm this popular belief. Imitation is almost instinctive in childhood, and children will readily imitate the strange sounds of a foreign language. Before adolescence they have not the inhibitions, the self-consciousness and the hesitations that make free verbal self-expression a difficult matter in many a secondary school classroom. It seems as though the organs of speech, the tongue and lips in particular, are more easily moulded in early childhood to the demands of the unfamiliar phonetics of a second language. Later on the muscles and mental processes used in speech become more set to the movements required for the mother tongue. These factors are, however, difficult to measure, and, though they are true enough, we must be careful not to over-rate their importance.

A persuasive theory in favour of an earlier start in language teaching has been advanced in the following terms.[2] It is

[1] *Modern Languages,* Ministry of Education pamphlet no. 29. H.M.S.O., 1956, p. 4.

[2] See H. Andersson, 'The Optimum Age for Beginning the Study of Modern Languages', in *International Review of Education,* Vol. 6, September 1960, pp. 298-306.

claimed that the language development of a child depends on *conditioned and conceptual* learning. Conditioned learning is the subconscious process which we described in Chapter 4, by which a child without conscious effort or reasoning is 'conditioned' by his experiences and circumstances to make certain linguistic performance. Conceptual learning on the other hand takes place when there is some conscious formation of concepts in the mind, when the child consciously perceives certain events, which lead to ideas in his mind and thus to certain purposeful behaviour on his part. The teaching of the mother tongue at secondary school stage involves very largely this kind of learning. The capacity for conditioned learning is at its maximum at birth or soon after and decreases from then on until it is comparatively small in adult life. Conceptual learning on the other hand is non-existent in the new born child, but steadily grows until it is the major factor in adult learning. From this it can be concluded that the best time for language learning would be those years when conditioned learning predominates, but when conceptual learning is becoming increasingly important. This would be the years before the age of ten. It is sometimes maintained that the optimum age for starting the learning of a foreign language would be that of four years, but the age of eight or thereabouts would seem to be a more practical suggestion. This psychological argument supposes that it is desirable to learn the foreign language in a way that would be somewhat similar to the learning of the native language, and the earlier it were undertaken the more it would be similar. It supposes too that conditioned learning needs to be used as much as possible in acquiring a foreign language, and this in turn involves the teaching of spoken language.

The activity methods commonly used in primary education today are particularly suited to this sort of teaching. Playing at the situations of real life, acting little scenes, imagining a whole situation—these are techniques frequently used by the primary school teacher and readily accepted by the primary school child. At this age the pupil will be quite happy to colour little drawings in his exercise book, to play counting games, to act out a scene at the classroom shop or to watch the performance of a glove puppet. Songs, games and drama are a familiar part of his school experience, and all these activities can be incorporated in the language lesson.

Bilingualism

In bilingual areas of the world children may learn two or more languages from an early age. This happens in certain parts of Wales, in the bilingual areas of Alsace and Belgium, and in various places in India and Africa, to mention only a few examples. The bilingual person learns to speak and understand two languages from infancy or childhood. We must remember that the truly ambilingual person, equally at home in both languages, is comparatively rare. Usually one language is preferred to the other, or the speaker may command a much wider range of vocabulary in one than the other. One language may be associated with one particular set of circumstances, it may be the home, and the other language may be reserved for a different set of situations, perhaps school or work. British children in imperial India would speak English to their parents, and Hindi, or some other vernacular, with almost equal ease to their ayah. In some parts of Wales children speak Welsh at home and English at school. In some foreign language teaching to younger children a conscious effort has been made to associate the foreign language with one classroom, suitably equipped and decorated for the purpose, and with one teacher, who practically always speaks in that language to the children.

Bilingualism shows that, given the opportunity, young children have a particular facility for learning more than one language, and for learning it through speech. There is no evidence to prove that bilingualism produces any harmful effects on the child's educational or mental development. Where bilingual children are found to be backward educationally, there are nearly always other factors, such as the effects of belonging to a social minority group, which are probably more powerful influences on the child's progress. Experience in Wales shows that young children can, in suitable circumstances, achieve fluent bilingualism with ease, and it seems that this is not at the expense of any other achievements of the child.[1]

Neurosurgery

The Canadian neurologist, Wilder Penfield, of McGill university, has made some definite pronouncements about language learning in childhood. He has studied the effects of brain damage, at various ages in life, on the language learning capacity of the individual. In cases where a child has suffered damage to that part of the brain concerned with speech, the child may become aphasic, but subsequently relearns the skills of speech. In the case of adults, however, once speech is lost through brain damage, full recovery is far less likely. Penfield claims that whereas in the case of the child the cerebral cortex has enough plasticity for another part of it to take over the functions of speech, no such readaptation is possible in the brain of the adult. He goes on to conclude that early childhood (the years before the age of ten) is the time when the human brain has the greatest facility for learning the skills of speech, and that therefore this is the time when persons can most easily learn to speak foreign languages. Although Penfield's theory is not universally accepted, this is an interesting piece of evidence in support of an earlier start on language learning.[2]

Developments in Other Countries

If we consider the question on the broadest possible front, we see that the large countries of Western Europe (especially Britain, France and Spain) have been rather unusual in not teaching a second language at this stage. When, in 1962, the Unesco Institute for Education in Hamburg held an international meeting on foreign languages in primary education, it was found that of the forty-five countries or regions for which the conference had information, thirty-two had some second language teaching in primary education below the age

[1] Further information on bilingualism is given in H. H. Stern, *Foreign Languages in Primary Education,* Unesco, 1963, Chapters 4 and 9.

[2] Penfield's views are given in Stern, *op. cit.,* Chapter 6. Stern discusses Penfield's ideas and gives references to his published work.

of ten. In many parts of the world the language situation is very different from that of the highly developed and linguistically unified countries of western Europe. In many countries of Africa it is assumed that either English or French must be learned from an early age, and consequently these languages are taught in primary schools. In Western Nigeria, for example, English lessons are introduced in the third term of the first year of primary schooling, and continue with increasing time allocation until in class five and above, all teaching except religious instruction is in English. In the non-Russian speaking parts of the U.S.S.R. Russian is taught as a second language from the first or second grade of primary education onwards. In western Europe, countries that have not one of the great world languages as the national tongue have developed language teaching in primary education considerably. German is started in the primary school in Luxembourg English has been taught in primary education in Sweden, and in the Netherlands French, German, English and Esperanto have all been taught at this stage. In French-speaking Switzerland German is a compulsory primary school subject, as French is in the Italian-speaking part of the country.

The general practice of starting foreign language teaching in United States high schools at about the ninth grade (age 14), and of running courses for two years only, has for some time been recognised as quite inadequate. Wide concern to improve language learning among Americans in the years following World War II led to attempts to teach languages at a much earlier age. So widespread were these experiments that in 1953 the U.S. Office of Education called a conference to discuss the question, 'Should foreign languages be taught in the elementary school?' The answer given by the conference delegates was emphatically 'Yes'. Since then the movement has developed in American schools and has been usually known as FLES (Foreign Languages in the Elementary School). A great deal of experiment has taken place in various parts of the United States, and yet only a small proportion of the total school population has so far been involved. The most popular starting age is eight to ten and the languages usually taught are Spanish, French and German. The greatest difficulty is the acute shortage of adequately qualified teachers for this type of work. Attempts have been made with television, film and other audio-visual courses to overcome this problem, and in some cases some excellent courses have been produced, as for example *Parlons Français,* which we considered in Chapter 5. Interesting and carefully evaluated work was done by Dunkel and Pillet at Chicago and has been well recorded in their book, *French in the Elementary School.* But in spite of excellent work in some places FLES as a whole has hardly been much of a success. The difficulty of finding suitable teachers, the inadequate supplies of materials, and frequently insufficient preparation for the courses have combined with the general remoteness of American schools from areas where languages other than English are spoken, to make the results of FLES somewhat disappointing. On the other hand, where experiments have been carefully carried out, as in the case of Dunkel and Pillet, the conclusion has been that FLES is a sound education proposition, which if carefully prepared and planned could be very successful.

In Sweden an experiment was started in 1957 in teaching English to children between the ages of seven and eleven by using audio-visual materials. The initiators of this experiment were Dr Gorosch, the Director of the Institute of Phonetics in the University of Stockholm, and Mr Axelsson, then Consultant for English teaching on the Swedish Board of Education, who together devised a course involving the use of tape-recordings and film-strips. With this material classes were taught English without reference to books and by teachers who had no special training in languages. The pupils spent fifteen minutes three times a week listening to the tapes and watching the pictures. Results were so encouraging that the course was further developed in the following years, until a full four-year course had been built up. There are many questions remaining which teachers and others working on this experiment in Sweden do not claim to have answered: the question of the optimum starting age, the amount of time needed for effective learning, the kind of vocabulary to be introduced, and so on. What does emerge from this work, however, confirms the view that foreign languages can successfully be taught to this age range. Even if the time devoted to such teaching is comparatively little—about fifteen minutes a day three times a week—useful results are obtained. It was found that pupils of eleven years of age learned more accurately and more quickly than the seven-year-olds. This does not of course mean that language learning ought not to be developed until the age of eleven, but it does show that facility for language learning is not necessarily greater the younger the child is. In fact it seems that a certain amount of conceptual learning entering into the process can speed and facilitate the learning of the L2. It is not possible, as we have already seen, to recapture completely the childhood conditions of L1 learning, and we must plan our teaching accordingly, even with younger children.

In 1962 the teaching of English became compulsory in Swedish schools from the fourth year of schooling upwards, that is from the age of ten. In the present system of comprehensive education, classes at that age are unstreamed and therefore English is taught to pupils of all levels of ability.

Experiments in language teaching to children under the age of ten have been made in certain other countries, notably in France, Western Germany and the U.S.S.R. Sometimes a foreign language has been introduced at the nursery school stage. All these experiments have had sufficient success to demonstrate clearly that young children can in fact learn a foreign language orally with considerable ease and proficiency. It is not too difficult to run a programme of language teaching in a limited number of primary schools and with a few good teachers. If, on the other hand, it is intended to introduce such teaching on anything like a national scale, problems of teacher training, of the provision of materials, and of continuity in the secondary schools, assume a magnitude that makes them nearly insurmountable. This is the difficulty that FLES has encountered and that has been a discouragement to the work in France. Countries such as those in Africa which need early language learning as a matter of national necessity in order to

lay the basis for secondary and higher education in English ‹
French, are obliged to overcome these difficulties. It become
assumed that a primary school teacher must be able to teacl
a second language, and that second language becomes a vita
part, indeed a predominant part, of primary schooling. In
Western European countries, as in U.S.A. and Australia, the
situation is different, and in these countries language teaching
must be planned nationally if it is to be effective at the primary
school level. Adequate provision must be made for the training
of teachers and for the supply of materials.

Changes within the Primary Schools

If we return now to the primary schools of Britain, we shall
find that within these schools themselves there are reasons
why the teaching of a foreign language should be developed
there. State elementary education in Britain, which grew so
extensively as a result of the Forster Act of 1870, was originally
thought of as a basic training in the three Rs for the children
of a certain section of the community. Men and women who
could read, write and reckon were needed for the semi-skilled
jobs in the factories and mills of England. Elementary education was concerned with providing this basic essential for the
masses of the people. In the economic and social circumstances
of the latter part of the nineteenth century it was not envisaged
that elementary education should go far beyond the basic
essentials. The children who were to learn Latin and Greek,
who would enter the ranks of the nation's doctors, lawyers,
administrators, engineers or scientists, were generally speaking
provided for in other schools.

Primary education nearly a hundred years later still provides
a basic training in the three Rs. But it does much more as well.
Not only is there such increased prosperity that we can afford
a much broader education for the children of all sectors of the
community, but we must also tap all the nation's manpower
resources to provide the large number of well-educated men
and women that the national economy requires. The role of
the primary schools has therefore changed. Education can be
planned at this level not simply in terms of minimal national

F

requirements, but to provide for the full development of the potential of each child. Teachers are better trained; a three-year course of training is now required for all, and an increasing number of graduates will teach in primary schools. Facilities and equipment in a modern well-planned primary school are luxurious by the standards of 1870. Starting from the immediate environment, the children of these schools are encouraged more and more to open their eyes on the world around them. Science in an introductory form is taught, and this is far more than the 'nature study' of former years. A well-stocked library of suitable books encourages the children to spread their interests farther afield, and to read about human life and activity the world over. School visits and journeys are arranged to places of interest not only in other parts of the country, but also, in some cases, abroad.

In this ever-widening scope of primary school interests it is clear that a purely monolingual culture cannot suffice indefinitely. Contact between national cultures is closer and more frequent now than it ever was, and children in school are more likely, in pursuing their interests, to meet the culture and language of other nations. If we are to encourage children to enquire into various aspects of the world around, there can be no justifiable educational reason for withholding from them the experience of meeting a foreign language at first hand. Everybody would like to promote understanding between nations, between peoples of differing race, religion and language, and everybody would probably agree that such understanding should be promoted at an early age. In this second half of the twentieth century it is likely that primary education will not continue to be based on the language of one national culture alone.

The reason usually given by primary school heads for including French in their curriculum, is that the children can learn a second language with enjoyment and profit; and if they can, it is an experience which they should not be denied. When one hears a class of nine-year-olds thoroughly enjoying an oral French lesson, and speaking simple French sentences with a high degree of accuracy and with poise, one can have no

doubt that this is in itself a good thing for them to do. It is educationally profitable at this stage, quite apart from the results it may yield in their language studies later on.

Some local education authorities are reorganising their schools so that one school will cover the age range nine to thirteen. No justification could remain in such circumstances for starting French, or any other foreign language, at eleven. The age would be purely arbitrary. Rather than delay second language learning until thirteen, it would be better in these schools to start it at nine.

We can see then that language teaching is not simply being imposed on primary schools from without; there is a call for it from within the schools. Indeed the developments within these schools make it more or less inevitable in the long run. But language teaching needs to be carefully planned and prepared, and should not be undertaken hastily or lightly. In some cases authorities have had to discourage schools from starting the teaching of French, lest in trying to be up-to-date and to provide for what they see is needed, the schools should fail through inadequate preparation or facilities.

Methods Used

Foreign language teaching in primary schools involves not only an earlier start, but a fresh approach to language teaching. The methods are different. The way in which we teach must be suited to the age of the learners. We cannot take secondary school language courses, methods, textbooks, and so on, and simply transpose them to the earlier age group. The spoken language is taught for some time before reading and writing are attempted. No formal grammar is taught at this stage, but learning is mainly by imitation and repetition. Children have a natural urge to imitate, and repetition is not so monotonous to them as it is to adults. The language is related to simple everyday situations in the home, the school, the shops, and so on. Full use is made of games, drama, song and the activity methods of the primary school, and audio-visual aids are used whenever the teacher considers them appropriate.

Let us imagine a class of about forty children aged eight or nine. They are seated at desks facing the teacher's table and the blackboard. The walls of the classroom are provided with colourful posters of France and scenes from French life. A tape-recorder is available near the teacher and a film-strip projector is ready for projecting pictures on a screen, which is to one side of the black-board, but visible to all the class. In one corner of the room a table is set out as a shop counter with various articles that might be purchased at a general store, or suitable replicas of these. The teacher has one or two glove puppets available on her desk. All this could well be regarded as the essential minimum equipment, and would certainly be provided in a special French-teaching room. If, as is more likely, the room is a general classroom, these things have to take their place alongside other displays and equipment for the teaching of other subjects.

Let us suppose now that we visit a class who have been learning French for only a few weeks. The teacher goes to the blackboard and draws the simple outline of a house. Then turning to the class she says several times, *Voici ma maison.* By means of a recognisable gesture she gets the class to repeat this phrase after her. Then she says, *Ma maison est petite,* and in the same way gets first the whole class and then certain individuals to repeat this, while with more than life-size gestures she makes clear the meaning of *petite.* In the same way she proceeds to *Ma maison est rouge, Voici la porte, La porte est bleue.* Colours are made clear by reference to a colour chart on the wall. If we add to this the question *Qu'est-ce que c'est?* and the answer *C'est la maison* or *C'est la porte,* this will be quite enough material for an oral lesson of twenty minutes or half an hour.

In subsequent lessons this will be developed with such phrases as, *Ma maison est près de l'église, Où est ma maison?, Est-elle bleue?* and so on. But all the time the teacher keeps a careful check of which sentence patterns have been introduced and these are frequently drilled by use. The pupils have notebooks in which they draw and colour a house, a door, a church, and so on. At any time when they are drawing, the teacher moves around among them and, pointing to a drawing in a notebook, asks the child individually *Qu'est-ce que c'est, Antoine?* The children are encouraged to ask questions of one another in a similar way in French. All these activities, if the teacher so wishes, can be undertaken in conjunction with an audio-visual course.

If we call again a few weeks later, we may find the same class engaged in oral work based on one of the posters. The class has already done a good deal of oral work on this in the manner already described. At the request of the teacher a pupil comes to the front and, pointing to various features in the picture displayed before the class, gives a description in these terms: *Voici un grand tableau. Dans le tableau il y a des champs et des arbres. Voici une ferme et voici une maison. La ferme est grande, mais la maison est petite. La maison est rouge. Il fait beau. Le soleil brille.* All these points are then revised by oral question and answer, or another pupil, one of the ablest in the class, comes to the front and asks questions about the picture to various pupils.

Later on pupils will be able to act little scenes involving simple conversation. One boy is the shopkeeper and stands behind the counter. A girl enters the shop with a cheery *Bonjour, monsieur,* and the conversation proceeds in this way, the children making appropriate actions:

Bonjour, madame, comment allez-vous?
Très bien, monsieur, et vous?
Oh! très bien, merci, madame. Vous désirez?
Un kilo de sucre, s'il vous plaît.
Voilà, madame. Et avec ça?
Une livre de beurre et un paquet de café, monsieur.
Voilà madame. C'est tout?
Oui, monsieur, c'est tout pour aujourd'hui.
C'est combien?
Sept francs cinquante, madame.
Voilà! Au revoir, monsieur.
Au revoir, madame, et merci.

Nobody who has heard a brief dialogue of this kind performed by primary school children can fail to be impressed. In so many cases the pronunciation is nearly perfect. The children catch the swing of the intonation and the speed and rhythm of the sentence that they have heard on the tape or from their teacher, and repeat it exactly with obvious pleasure. They know little or nothing of grammar. To them the language is a meaningful means of expression, a genuine alternative to the mother tongue.

We might wonder how some of these phrases have been taught. *Comment allez-vous?* for example, is a sentence, the meaning of which cannot be conveyed so easily as in the case of *la porte est bleue.* The audio-visual course is a great help here and offers many opportunities for teaching meaning. But it is also surprising how much can be done by pure Direct Method techniques in a normal classroom situation. At other times the teacher may resort to English, not exactly giving a translation, but explaining beforehand in English what is to be the significance of the French to follow, a system used by *Tavor.* Taking a glove puppet the teacher may say: 'Now I am meeting this fellow in the street; he asks me how I am, and I say I am very well. Then of course I add, "And how are you?" He says he is very well too'. She then proceeds with the first part of the conversation in the above dialogue, as an imagined conversation between herself and the glove puppet, She herself speaking both parts. In these and other ingenious ways teachers manage to convey the meaning of the unfamiliar words. These procedures and other similar ones have been well described by L. R. Cole,[1] who admirably presents the subtleties and the pitfalls of these teaching methods.

The Work in the Schools

A few years ago considerable publicity was given to an experiment in teaching French in primary schools in Leeds. This has been fully described elsewhere,[2] and there is no need to give a detailed account of it here. In 1961 a specially selected

[1] L. R. Cole, *Teaching French to Juniors,* University of London Press, 1964.

[2] M. Kellermann, *Two Experiments on Language Teaching in Primary Schools in Leeds,* The Nuffield Foundation, Nuffield Lodge, Regent's Park, London N.W.1, 1964. Further information is also available in articles that have appeared in *Education,* 5 January 1962, 24 August 1962, and 25 January 1963.

group of Leeds children, aged ten and eleven, worked for most of each school day on learning French, and learning other subjects in French, with a gifted French-speaking teacher. Results were so encouraging that the work was extended in the following year to other schools, and now it is the objective of the Leeds education authority that every child in the city schools should have the opportunity to learn spoken French in the final year of primary schooling. Even before the work started in Leeds, some Blackpool primary schools had been teaching French. Under the influence of Mr S. R. Ingram, one of the first teachers to use the *Tavor* course, the teaching of French started in East Ham. Then in various places all over the country language teaching at this level rapidly developed. In 1963 a survey was made by Mr C. M. Lazaro, for the Nuffield Foundation, of language teaching in primary schools throughout Great Britain.[1] At that time Lazaro estimated that there were at least 280 primary schools (200 in England and 80 in Scotland) which were then, or soon would be, engaged in foreign language teaching.

Since that year the Schools Council's pilot scheme for foreign language teaching in primary schools has been launched involving thirteen areas and forty-eight associated areas. Some local authorities, such as Bournemouth and Wakefield, since they have not been included in the Council's pilot scheme, are developing their own plans for primary school French and making their own provision for the training of teachers. German is being taught successfully in primary schools in East Sussex, and in Glasgow French teaching in some primary schools by using closed-circuit television is being developed under a specially appointed organiser. A vast movement throughout the country is gathering momentum. In some cases, no doubt, schools are simply leaping on the latest bandwaggon, but this cannot be said of the thorough and painstaking work proceeding in many areas.

On the question of the quality of the work the Lazaro report

[1] C. M. Lazaro, *Report on Foreign Language Teaching in British Primary Schools, January to March* 1963. Mimeographed by the Nuffield Foreign Languages Teaching Materials Project, 1963.

of 1963 had some hard things to say. Lazaro himself visited ninety-five schools in a wide variety of areas where this work was going on, and in these schools 144 teachers were involved in foreign language teaching. Of these teachers 100 had no formal qualifications for language teaching; nineteen only had degrees in the modern languages concerned, and two only had taken a language as a special subject at a training college. 119 of these teachers had no previous experience of teaching a foreign language. Almost half the 144 teachers whose classes were visited could have profited from instruction in the use of the language. On the question of teaching techniques, Lazaro, who himself is an experienced languages teacher from the Argentine, was of the opinion that twelve teachers out of the 144 could be described as excellent, a further forty-two as good. 'Many of the remainder,' he went on, 'displayed various faults of method and class management, and their teaching showed a need for specialist training and advice.' [1] Not always were the best linguists the best teachers, and the provision of audio-visual aids did not necessarily make the teaching good.

In assessing the results achieved by the classes he observed, Lazaro graded the classes on a scale A to D, which indicated a range from excellent to sub-standard. Of 150 classes observed, 14 were assessed at A, 28 at B, 19 at C and 89 at D. It is noticeable on this classification that the younger classes tended to do better in proportion than the older ones, and five of the fourteen classes in the A category were in fact infant school classes.

This report is in itself most interesting, but is of course a personal and, to a large extent, subjective appraisal. The situation has changed considerably since 1963. Nevertheless, the dangers are clear enough. It was found in Leeds that teachers must be good to be of any real value in this work. If success is to be reached, much more experimenting needs to be done, much more provision must be made for training the teachers, and the whole question of continuity in the secondary school needs to be exhaustively examined and carefully organised. These things and others the Lazaro report called for urgently.

[1] Lazaro, *op. cit.*, p. 6.

Criticisms and Doubts

It is appropriate here that we should consider some of the criticisms of language teaching in primary schools that have been expressed, and some of the doubts about it that certainly lurk in many minds. Criticisms have come from teachers in secondary schools, especially grammar schools, who fear that a wholesale change in the starting age for language learning is going to upset the established and well-tried pattern of language teaching in British schools. In this fear they are probably justified, but provided a better pattern results from the change, there could be no valid objection. We must be prepared for considerable upheaval and for new and unorthodox views of language teaching in education.

We might wonder if language learning is going to constitute too heavy a burden on children of eight to eleven years old. Will this extra subject prejudice their opportunities of success in other aspects of their school work? All the results of experiments so far disprove any suggestion of a burden. Children enjoy the work immensely, and there have been a number of cases where success in the foreign language has given a child such a sense of achievement, that the self-confidence engendered has carried over to other subjects, and in these the pupils work has improved. In Leeds the children who have worked on French in the final year at primary school have not done any worse in the eleven-plus examination. Studies of bilingualism show, as we have seen, that the use of two languages has no harmful educational consequences. The Welsh Federation of Head Teachers, in submitting evidence to the Plowden committee, stated that children brought up bilingually incur no educational disadvantages, and some evidence even suggests that they may do better than monoglot children.

Secondary school teachers fear that errors, especially errors of pronunciation, learned in the primary school may be impossible to eradicate from the child's speech at a later stage. This may well be so, in fact it is certain to happen in some cases. The fear, however, reflects a lack of confidence in primary school teachers. However much this may apparently be justified by the Lazaro survey, or other evidence, the real solution is not to oppose the teaching of languages in primary schools for this reason, but to press for better training of language teachers for these schools.

A more subtle and more serious criticism concerns the nature of the child's learning. It is undeniable that within certain limitations primary school children have learned to speak French. But it is sometimes objected that this knowledge is little more than a parrot-like repetition of certain set speech patterns that have constantly occurred in classroom work. When the child is required to adapt this knowledge to new situations, it is said, he is at a loss to reconstruct from his knowledge new speech patterns that are appropriate to the new situations. This criticism may be valid for many of the children concerned, but this does not mean that their learning of French is faulty. We must be very careful here not to expect of children mental processes that are inappropriate to their age. Children up to the age of eleven have not the mental capacity to manipulate certain abstract conceptions, which may be a normal part of the thinking of adults. Even without teaching grammatical abstractions explicitly, we may be demanding of the child a kind of mental process that is beyond him. For example, the average eleven-year-old is unable to analyse a sentence into clauses; the syntactical relationship of clauses to one another involves conceptions which do not enter into his normal thinking. Even in his mother tongue his speech is largely composed of main clauses and a limited range of tenses. To ask him to manipulate a foreign language in a way that is beyond his mental powers provides no basis for criticising his language learning. In fact we need to know far more about the language of children and about what abilities they have to manipulate language. If children of seven or eight cannot progress beyond the repetitive stage of language learning, we might wonder whether time spent by them on learning a foreign language is well spent at all. They could perhaps get through this repetitive stage and reach a stage of manipulation more rapidly if they started learning a language at eleven. Some of the experience in Sweden suggests this. But it would appear that any child has the ability at any given time to reach the same level of achievement in a foreign language as he has reached at that time in his mother tongue. Bilingualism shows that nearly equal achievement in two languages is possible. In all probability we should be very patient about repetitive learning; it may be that this type of learning must go on in young children for a good many years of their development. Only detailed studies of children's language and of the thought processes behind their language can show us accurately what degree of linguistic manipulation can be expected of a child at any given age.

Other objections concern the knowledge of the written language. Some grammar schools have found that pupils who had learned French in their primary schools, had considerable ability in speaking, but were inaccurate in writing French. How are we to evaluate the work of an eleven-year-old pupil who can write two pages of fluent French on, shall we say, the Roman conquest of Gaul? His French vocabulary is quite good, he can express himself well in written French, but his work is well scattered with errors of spelling and agreement and with a few mistakes of syntax. Is it fair to compare this with an essay from, say, a seventeen-year-old pupil who has had several years of schooling in the finer points of grammar, but who may be tongue-tied in oral expression? If we compare it with the efforts of eleven-year-old pupils who have done no French in the primary school it is vastly better, and shows a far wider experience in the language. We may find that the errors are more like those that would be made by a French pupil of comparable age writing in his mother tongue. If pupils learn to speak the language before they write it, it is almost inevitable that they will be more fluent than accurate when they come to write. This situation need cause no surprise; it is simply a little different from what grammar schools have been accustomed to. If French pupils of eleven make mistakes in written French which they later overcome, there is no reason why English pupils learning French should not also overcome such mistakes. The most important thing is that the basic structures of the language should be there in the mind and that the basic skills and habits of speech should be acquired. The refinements of written accuracy can be learned later.

Two Projects

The teaching of languages in primary schools is being very considerably assisted by two schemes which were announced by the Minister of Education in March 1963. These are the Nuffield Foundation Foreign Languages Teaching Materials Project and the pilot scheme which has now become the responsibility of the Schools Council. From the start the Nuffield Foundation had supported the experimental work in Leeds, but it soon became clear that very extensive work would need to be done in providing teaching materials if the teaching of languages in primary schools was to make any real progress. The Foundation decided to finance a project for the production of such materials for language teaching to the eight to thirteen age range. Mr A. Spicer, of the Department of Phonetics of Leeds University, was seconded to direct the project and under him was appointed a staff of teachers, linguists, artists and others, who would develop the materials required. The first task of Mr Spicer's team has been the production of an audio-visual French course, which we have considered in Chapter 5. From September 1964 onward the prototype of this course has been available to schools participating in the pilot scheme of the Schools Council. But before detailed work started on this course, a full survey was made of all audio-visual French courses suitable for primary schools which were available at the time. An annotated bibliography was published which gives detailed information on all the courses considered.[1] The Nuffield Project has also initiated a survey of the language of English-speaking children, while CREDIF has started a similar survey of the language of French-speaking children. The results of these surveys will be most valuable in designing courses which will teach children, as far as possible, the kind of language appropriate to their age. The Project has also produced a

[1] See note 1, p. 87.

number of publications of interest and help to teachers, including an up-to-date catalogue of the books and audio-visual aids in the Project's reference library, which also serves as a working bibliography for the teaching of French as a foreign language in various types of schools. The Project was later extended to provide materials for the teaching of Spanish, German and Russian to pupils aged eleven to thirteen. Audio-visual courses in these languages are being prepared and will be published from 1967 onwards.[1]

The Schools Council's pilot scheme was intended to discover what the implications would be, both from an educational and administrative point of view, of the introduction of French teaching into the primary schools as a matter of national policy. It was intended to support the teaching of French in primary schools in certain selected areas, so that results of this work could be carefully assessed. All local education authorities were sent a letter detailing the aims of the scheme and the conditions required. The experiment had to be controlled, and there had to be adequate continuity between primary and secondary schools. Over sixty authorities applied for full membership of the scheme of which thirteen were finally selected, representing various parts of the country and various types of neighbourhood. A number of other authorities were granted associate membership.

Member authorities were free to decide which of their schools and teachers should participate in the scheme, but it was stipulated that the first essential was good primary school teachers; a good French speaker who was an indifferent teacher would not do. There was to be no central control over methods of teaching, though these were to be fully discussed and recommendations made. The local authorities could call on help from the Department of Education and Science and from local H.M.I.s, as this might be needed. But the Department's principal function here was to train teachers for the work. Most of the teachers involved were trained before September 1964, in two training courses in Paris and two in Besançon,

[1] Further information about the work of the Nuffield Project may be obtained from the Information Officer, 31 Harrogate Road, Leeds 7.

each of three months' duration. Three ten-day courses on methodology were also held in England. Some local training courses were also provided and were run by the local authorities.

These two projects are complementary. The Nuffield Project provides the materials for the Schools Council's scheme, which in turn provides the schools and the teachers who can use, assess and suggest improvements for the Nuffield materials. We have seen that the two great needs for this work on a national scale are the provision of materials and the training of teachers. These are being catered for in the two projects. Furthermore, we have here a scheme for carefully controlled experiment which the Lazaro report had called for, in view of a sober assessment of the possibilities and problems of primary school language teaching on a national scale.

Conclusions

The National Foundation for Education Research has been entrusted with the task of evaluating the Schools Council's Project of language teaching in primary schools. Though we cannot anticipate the Foundation's findings, it seems certain now that primary school French has come to stay. Language teaching has become too firmly established in many primary schools to be abandoned completely. In any case the schools like it, and want it, and are doing it well. We have traced in this chapter the various lines of thought that have led to the development of this teaching, so that we can now see that we are concerned with an educational trend of considerable importance. But while it is certain that primary school French will not be abandoned, there are nonetheless many questions related to this matter which are not nearly so certain. We must await the conclusion of the first stage of the pilot scheme, which is to run from 1964 to 1969, before we know whether foreign language teaching in primary schools is to be adopted on a national scale or whether it is to remain a development in some areas only. The starting age is also a matter of uncertainty. The Schools Council's scheme and the Nuffield project favour the age of eight. But, owing to the difficulty of finding enough teachers of the right kind, Leeds is keeping to a starting age of ten. The age at which writing should be introduced is a point that is equally important, but which we have hardly touched on here. Whether teachers should be specialists or class-teachers is a further point of difficulty. These and other questions can only be solved with time and experience.

Among these questions there are three that stand out. They are the problems of continuity, of providing materials and of training teachers. The first of these we shall deal with more fully in Chapter 9. The provision of materials is being largely catered for by the Nuffield Project. It is the training of teachers that presents the greatest problem. The expansion of colleges of education and the increase in the number of colleges offering a main course in a modern language is most significant here, and we shall say more of this in our chapter on the universities and teacher training. But clearly in-service training must be developed much more, as in the Schools Council's pilot scheme. If primary school language teaching is to be developed nationally on any really serious scale, many thousands of teachers will have to be trained for the work. This factor will undoubtedly limit the speed with which a national policy can be implemented.

Perhaps the most interesting prospect afforded by the project is the possibility of rejuvenating the whole system of language teaching from the bottom up. Instead of being dead, instead of being drudgery—as it has been in some cases—language learning could become something to be enjoyed. It could become practical and realistic, related to real life, meaningful. The upsurge from the primary schools must ultimately permeate the whole secondary school system. There are exciting prospects of real change.

9

Implications for Secondary Schools

As we turn our attention now to secondary schools, we find that in them all the various lines of development that we have been considering converge. Audio-visual courses and language laboratories are being offered to these schools, which in many cases are gladly accepting new methods and new ideas. The primary schools in some areas are beginning to feed the secondary schools with pupils who have already an appreciable knowledge of the spoken language. New types of examinations, looming ahead, offer fresh objectives and fresh challenges. At the same time it is in the secondary schools that traditionally the largest proportion of the country's language teaching has been done. It is they that have the qualified language teachers in large numbers; it is they that have the experience in language teaching. The crucial and interesting question is how these schools are going to react to the new forces in language teaching within and around them.

The Reorganisation of Secondary Education
In the years that followed the passing of the 1944 Education Act it became increasingly apparent that the tripartite system of secondary education involving selection at eleven plus was unsatisfactory for the nation as a whole. Many experiments in other ways of organising education took place, and the matter eventually entered the field of politics when the Labour Party committed itself to comprehensive education in principle. More recently a large number of local education authorities have developed some form of comprehensive education, often of a two-tier kind with a change of school at

age thirteen or fourteen. On 12 July 1965 the Secretary of State for Education and Science issued Circular 10/65 calling upon all local authorities to submit within a year plans for the reorganisation of secondary education in their areas along comprehensive lines. Various ways of doing this were suggested in the circular. There might be the orthodox comprehensive school for all pupils between the ages of eleven and sixteen or eighteen. There might be two-tier comprehensive schools with a change of school at age thirteen or fourteen, or various modifications of this, as for example the Leicestershire pattern. There might be a common school for pupils aged eleven to sixteen and then a sixth-form college. Finally, it is now possible to have a scheme involving a middle school for the age range nine to thirteen and a comprehensive secondary school for pupils aged thirteen and upwards. Whatever plan may be adopted, all these various possibilities involve the end of selection at eleven (though some schemes retain a measure of selection at thirteen or fourteen) and a system of comprehensive education for all. This means that the old distinction between grammar school and secondary modern school will disappear altogether in the course of the next decade.

This holds some important implications for modern language teaching. First, the distinction between grammar and secondary modern schools meant there was one type of school that taught one modern language to practically all its pupils and a second or third language to a few, and that there was also a type of school where only a minority of the pupils, if any, learned a modern language at all. This distinction is now to go. It will become increasingly difficult to avoid the conclusion that a modern language should be taught to all pupils, both the able and the less able. If there is to be ease of transfer within the comprehensive school there must be a common curriculum in the early years; only some such system will give equality of opportunity. The development of modern languages tests in the new C.S.E. examinations means that it is expected that a language will be taught to pupils of only average or slightly less than average ability. Audio-visual aids are providing much greater facilities for such teaching than have existed in the past. In this connection the Swedes have shown us an example of how a foreign language can form part of the curriculum of every child in a comprehensive school.[1] In any case, in areas where French is being taught to the full ability range in the primary school, it is clearly intended that all these pupils should continue the subject at the secondary stage. When this is so there is no logical reason for refraining from teaching French to any pupil in a secondary school, whether he started the language in the primary school or not.

This was clearly seen by the authors of the Newsom report, who saw a great potential value in learning a foreign language for the pupils of average or less than average ability, whose education they were considering. The report states that learning a foreign language has an important connection with the need for improved powers of communication in these children. It might give confidence to the diffident, and might open 'one more window on the world' by enabling pupils to communicate directly with a foreign people. The use of audio-visual aids and language teaching in primary schools were seen as trends which favour this development. The report adds: 'Given good conditions, a foreign language, taught by a well-conceived oral course and enlivened wherever possible by direct contacts with a foreign country, might well be one of the most stimulating subjects in the curriculum for some of the pupils of this report'.[2]

It is intended to raise the school leaving age to sixteen in 1970-71. This will further extend the range of modern language teaching in secondary schools. It will then be possible to plan a five-year course for all pupils who study a foreign language, to which must be added, for some at least, time spent on learning a language before this in the primary school. A five-year course should offer real possibilities for the non-academic child to become acquainted with the spoken language within certain limits. But, as the Newsom Report and the Schools Council's working paper on *Raising the School Leaving Age* have pointed out, there is relatively little

[1] See p. 150.

[2] *Half Our Future* (Newsom Report), H.M.S.O., 1963, p. 163.

experience in teaching a foreign language over the whole, or even most of the ability range. For the time being the Schools Council is concentrating its attention on the eight to thirteen age group in matters of language teaching, but in the next few years much more will need to be done in developing the possibilities of teaching what Mr George Taylor has called *Les Langues Non-Scolaires*[1] beyond the age of thirteen and in providing the teachers for the task.

In language teaching in comprehensive secondary schools we shall probably have to distinguish various levels of teaching according to the ability of the pupils. We can discern three of these levels, though these might be subdivided into others. There are first of all the able pupils who will take and pass G.C.E. Ordinary level. These pupils may learn by audio-visual methods and by work in a language laboratory, but they will not only learn the spoken language; they will also be expected to master the written language and may go on to more advanced studies in the subject at sixth-form and university levels. Second, there will be those pupils who are entered for the C.S.E. examination, some of whom may be every bit as successful as are those in the first group. But in the main these pupils will not be expected to develop so great a command of the written language, though they will learn to express themselves in simple form in writing. A very large amount of their work will relate to oral communication only. Third, there will be a group of pupils who will never write the language with any accuracy and probably never read it very much. But they will become acquainted with certain common expressions and a limited vocabulary which will enable them to speak about the most elementary matters, especially to persons of comparable ability and background in the foreign country. This suggests a totally different teaching objective from that involved in traditional grammar school teaching. It may be very difficult for teachers of long experience in grammar schools to adapt themselves to this fresh type of teaching.

[1] G. Taylor, 'Les Langues Non-Scolaires', in *Modern Languages*, Vol. XLVII, No. 1, March 1966.

The second result for language teaching of the reorganisation of secondary education is that, in cases where a two-tier system is adopted, it will not be possible for one and the same teacher to take a pupil right through from his first lesson in the subject to the Ordinary level examination. Nor will it be possible for one Head of Department to organise and supervise the whole course. There will be a break and a change of both teacher and school. There has, of course, very often been a change of teacher at some point in the secondary school course, but yet it has been possible to plan the course as one whole with some continuity in matters of textbooks and methods. There can still be such continuity, but this will now involve cooperation with teachers in other schools. The Head of Department in a senior high school will need to arrange his syllabus in consultation with language teachers in the junior high school from which pupils come at the age of thirteen or fourteen. The teaching of French in primary schools is bringing about a similar situation in any case, quite apart from secondary reorganisation. Secondary teachers who receive pupils from primary schools where French is taught have to plan their teaching so that there is continuity. No longer can the secondary school languages teacher rejoice that his pupils come to him knowing nothing of the subject and that therefore, unlike his colleagues who teach mathematics or English, he is not building on another's shaky foundation, but is laying the foundation himself. Now, in very many secondary schools the position will be changed; the pupils will have started the subject elsewhere.

The Forces of Change

There are three converging forces at present affecting language teaching in secondary schools. In some schools these forces may not be felt at all. In others only one or two of them may be operating. There seems little doubt, however, that ultimately all three will have a profound influence on the very nature of language teaching in the secondary schools as they are evolving under various types of reorganisation. The first of these forces is represented by the considerable number of pupils from primary schools who are now in various areas proceeding to secondary schools with some considerable knowledge of French or of some other language acquired in the primary school. The second is the influence of new types of examinations, both the new C.S.E. examination and new types of Ordinary level which are beginning to develop. The third force, and perhaps the most widespread, is in the introduction of new methods and new courses within the secondary schools themselves; here we have in particular the use of audio-visual and audio-lingual courses and the establishment of language laboratories. We have already considered each one of these factors in Part Two and in the preceding chapter. Now, in the next three sections of this chapter, we are going to examine the effects of each of these in the teaching that takes place and will take place in the schools. There may be other forces as well, such as the requirements of industry, but the three we are considering are probably the most important at present.

We must notice here that each of these three forces is tending in the same direction. Though they have developed to some extent independently, they do not conflict. Each of these three movements gives much greater prominence to the spoken language; each involves a conception of language as primarily a matter of oral communication; each is a movement in favour of learning by oral practice, rather than by the study of grammar and by exercises in translation. No doubt in all this the indirect influence of linguistics and psychology is felt, since advances in these academic fields have very largely influenced thought about language teaching in connection with present-day developments. Each of the three forces that we are considering is really part of one great movement of change that is gradually but surely taking place.

Continuing Primary School Work

The secondary school teacher who is confronted with a group of first-form pupils fresh from learning French in their primary school, could if he wished pour scorn on their achievements. He could prove to them that they knew hardly anything about tenses, that they could not conjugate irregular verbs, that they could not translate even simple passages into French, in fact by certain standards it might be said that they knew hardly any French after perhaps one or two years' work in the subject. This would, of course, be to overlook the fact that they could express themselves orally in simple sentences, that they could understand quite a bit of spoken French, and that they could hold a simple conversation about some everyday matters within strict limits of vocabulary and sentence structure. Even a teacher who spoke appreciatively to the pupils about the work they had done at their previous school, might proceed to teach by such dull, grammatical methods that the pupils' interest would wane and all the advantage they had gained from oral work in the primary school would be lost. There must clearly be a sympathetic understanding of what the primary school has been seeking to achieve. The secondary school languages teacher must make himself acquainted with the work done in the primary schools, with the methods and audio-visual courses used and with the aims and objectives of primary school language teaching. Second, he must learn how to continue in the first-year class in the same sort of way. He must follow methods of oral work familiar to the pupils and keep alive in them the ability in simple oral communication that they have already acquired. Third, he must learn how to develop true grammatical knowledge from this basis of oral skills, and how to consolidate an ability in the written language without in any way jeopardising those same oral skills.

Primary school French does of course create organisational problems in the secondary school. For a good many years to come there are likely to be schools that receive a mixed bag of eleven plus entrants; some will have done French and some will have done none, and of those that have done some French there may be wide variety in the length of time spent on the language and the standard reached. There may be cases where a school develops such close cooperation with the primary schools that feed it, that an even standard will be arrived at in French teaching to all ten-year-olds. Even in such a case differences of ability and other factors will make for a great range of achievement. The familiar situation will probably be that secondary schools will face a year-group of whom some will have reached a good standard in French, some will have done no more than a little and some will have done none at all. By streaming or setting it will be possible in most cases to get a complete class of pupils who have done a good deal of work in the language. According to the size of the intake and other factors there may be one, two or more such classes. Similarly there may be one or more classes of pupils who have done no French. These of course present the traditional situation and hardly call for special comment. There will also be classes including some pupils who have done primary school French and some who have not. Here the teacher faces a real problem. By some teachers this challenge has been faced very successfully. Clearly a special technique has to be devised to meet the special requirements of such a class. It will be necessary to start at the beginning, since some pupils will know no French at all. Those who know French already can be used in simple oral exchanges and repetitions from which the rest of the class can learn. With part of the class knowing some French the remainder should learn more rapidly than would a class consisting entirely of beginners. At every successive stage, as additional vocabulary and structures are introduced, the same procedure would be used. The French speakers would engage in oral work with the teacher while the others would listen. Gradually at each stage the whole class would be brought in. Work in reading and writing would be introduced almost from the beginning of the first year to provide further interest and challenge for those who had done so much of the oral work before. Some careful planning along these lines would make the most of the opportunities afforded by a first-year class of mixed composition.

What then are the methods of teaching that should be adopted in the secondary school in order to provide adequate continuity with primary school language teaching? First, there must be an abundance of well-planned oral work. In the last chapter we described how primary children can learn to talk about a poster-size picture of a French scene. This sort of oral activity can be carried on in the first year of the secondary school in exactly the same way. The pupils will also be accustomed to acting little scenes involving the simple conversation of the home, the street or the shop. If this is done in the initial stages at the secondary school, the pupils will feel they are continuing the work done previously, which indeed they are, and will thus grow in confidence. The teacher meanwhile will have ample opportunity of assessing his new pupils and judging their linguistic performance.

These simple beginnings can be gradually developed into fresh experiences. The pictures and dramatic sketches could be built up into a body of information about a foreign family or school or town, either imaginary or real. The children could come to think about the members of an imaginary family, and in each lesson something fresh might happen to these characters. This sort of idea has been basic to many of the traditional coursebooks in use in schools today. There is no need however to have a coursebook for this work to be done. All the simple incidents of family meals, leaving home for school, meeting friends in the street, and so on could be acted in the classroom, so that the pupils build up a knowledge of the phrases appropriate to these situations.

At the same time the oral work could be developed by the introduction of some elementary pattern practice. Chorus responses could be required, or individual answers from certain pupils. Such exercises should be simple. It will be better to oversimplify, so that the pupil can hardly get anything wrong. These drills will probably be new to the pupils, so that they will feel they are tackling something fresh, yet at the same time they will be consolidating grammar work already covered. As the approach is entirely oral, this will not only provide continuity of method, but will draw on all that these pupils have acquired in the way of pronunciation and fluency over the previous year or two.

In the second place the secondary school teacher can continue the primary school work by making use of an audio-visual course. This could be a course such as the B.B.C. *French* for *Beginners* or *Longmans Audio-Visual French,* though both of these assume that the pupil has not done French before. If *Bonjour Line!* had been used in the primary school, pupils might continue with *Voix et Images de France,* but this is really designed for adults. It is probably only in the Nuffield course that there could be really excellent continuity. Since this is to cover the age range eight to thirteen, we can assume that pupils who start the course in the primary school could continue with it in the first two years of secondary school. In any case pupils accustomed to the audio-visual method of learning should continue to work with this method in some way.

Third, the secondary school teacher will do well to make as much use as possible of supplementary audio-visual and aural material. The B.B.C. sound programmes for schools in French or German will be particularly valuable for pupils who have started to learn one of these languages in the primary school. Some simple sound films such as those that have been produced to accompany the CREDIF audio-visual courses, or those in the well-known *La Famille Martin* series[1], might well be used at some suitable point in the early years of the secondary school course, to supplement the normal classroom work, and to keep alive that sense of the reality of the language that will have been fostered in the primary school. Where a French 'assistant' is available in the school, he could be used extensively in oral work in the classroom with these pupils who are already accustomed to speaking French and hearing it spoken. Far too often the 'assistant' is used only with senior classes for so-called conversation work. There are in fact enormous possibilities in using the foreign speaker in the classroom at the same time as the normal teacher. Under the guidance and direction of the latter, the 'assistant' could conduct oral exercises, take part in some dramatic sketches with the pupils or initiate simple conversational dialogues .

It is in the secondary school, and especially in the classes of good ability, that we shall expect to see a real consolidation of

[1] Supplied by the Educational Foundation for Visual Aids, 33 Queen Anne Street, London, W.1.

grammatical knowledge and a development of written skills. There is no reason for any neglect of this side of the work; on the contrary, we can hope for a better understanding of grammar than previously. Ideally, the language learner should be familiar with structures and forms in spontaneous oral work, before he proceeds to study the grammar as an abstraction. He should, for example, be using the various parts of *être* and *avoir* quite freely and correctly before the conjugation of the present tense of these verbs is formally presented to him as an abstraction. This would be a truly inductive method of grammar teaching, and would resemble more closely the teaching of the grammar of the mother tongue. We may be too idealistic in hoping for this, but the success of some work in primary schools seems to indicate that this is not beyond the bounds of possibility. It should be possible for the teacher to start a grammar lesson on the possessive adjective in French by saying something like this: 'You know already that we say *Mon livre est bleu, Ma règle est cassée* and *Mes cahiers sont dans le pupitre.* Let us think about why we use *mon* in some cases, *ma* in other cases, and sometimes *mes*'. There would of course be much more to the opening of the lesson than just these words, but the teacher could appeal to knowledge already acquired by the pupils and develop and deepen it through grammatical study.

The Place of Audio-visual Courses

It would seem evident now that audio-visual language teaching courses are more appropriate in some teaching situations than in others. We considered some of these courses in Chapter 5; we are now attempting to assess their place and importance in secondary education. Already we have seen that an audio-visual course may be valuable in keeping alive the oral ability in the language that may have been developed in the primary school. This is an example of a situation where such a course can be used to great advantage. In other situations this type of course, indeed this whole approach to language learning, may not be appropriate. The sixth-form languages specialists probably do not need an audio-visual course. This is not because they are not concerned with the spoken language, but rather because the sort of thing they must be encouraged to say in the language does not lend itself to visual representation. On the whole we shall find that audio-visual courses are more appropriate with younger pupils and in the early stages of learning a language. This may mean that we shall expect to find audio-visual courses more used in junior high schools than in senior high schools. But in the present state of our knowledge about such techniques of teaching it would be rash to make any rigid dictum on such a subject.

It may also be found that the audio-visual approach is very suited to pupils of less than average ability. The visual element provides a practical situation to which language can be related, and when such a situation is depicted, the spoken language may be more readily grasped than the written mode would be, with its additional complications of orthography, agreement and so on. However, certain enquiries into television viewing seem to indicate that in some cases the visual so much predominates in the mind that the spoken word can go unheeded. If this happened in the audio-visual language classroom almost no language would be learned. More research is needed to establish the relative value of these media with different types of mind.

In the same way we may well wonder how language laboratory methods are suited to various ages or abilities. Although the language laboratory has been used successfully with quite young children,[1] this approach to language teaching has become more associated with adult or near-adult learners. The degree of perseverance required, the need for working in the relative isolation of the booth, the often abstract nature of the concepts lying behind the drills, all this would seem to indicate that this type of work is for the adult rather than for the child. Hilton alloted a considerable amount of time in the laboratory at Chorley to first-year languages classes. This may be very successful, but it is mainly in middle-school years that the difficult grammatical structures of French and German need

[1] D. Robinson, 'Eight-year-olds in the Language Laboratory', in *Visual Education,* October 1962.

to be systematically drilled. This is surely where laboratory exercises can really help. It is in fact with adult beginners, or near-beginners, in technical colleges that language laboratories have been even more extensively used, and it is with such learners that impressive results have been obtained. When we come to the post-Ordinary-level stage we shall need to think further about the types of exercise to be used. No doubt the laboratory can be very useful in improving pupils' advanced knowledge of conversation, in making more detailed studies of intonation and in developing greater speed and fluency. In the realm of literature there are considerable possibilities for teaching poetry and drama, as well as prose literature, with the help of language laboratory recordings. At undergraduate level these same considerations would apply. As teaching becomes more advanced and more specialised, there is a tendency for students to work as individuals rather than as classes. At sixth-form and university level students often require more individual attention and a course tailor-made for the needs of the individual or the small group. This is the sort of work that can be provided for in the language laboratory.

For these reasons we may expect that language laboratories may be established ultimately in all schools and colleges providing language teaching for older adolescents and adults. Audio-visual courses may be appropriate for such learners in many cases, but they will on the whole be more extensively used in primary schools and in the early years of secondary schooling. The reorganisation of secondary education on the two-tier system may encourage the pattern of predominantly audio-visual courses in junior high schools and language laboratories, with or without a visual aid, in senior high schools.

Perhaps the most serious misgivings about the use of these new techniques in secondary schools concerns the possible effects on standards of written work. Experience tends to show that the methods of teaching languages used in primary schools and audio-visual methods employed in secondary schools, while they may greatly improve pupils' performance in oral-aural skills, do also result in a lowering of standards of accuracy in writing in the language, at the stage when this is learned. Advocates of the new techniques would like to think that this is only temporary and that by the time our pupils, taught by the new techniques, have reached the fourth or fifth year in the secondary school, they will have acquired mastery of the writing skills in addition to the speaking skills, and all is well. But this is by no means certain. While the present form of Ordinary level remains, no conscientious grammar school teacher can allow any change in written standards, and yet many are adopting audio-visual courses, and some are using language laboratories. Somehow means are being found of safeguarding the standards of written work. This may be at the expense of a fully-fledged audio-visual method; which is really no more than further evidence of the way wise and experienced teachers can adapt new developments in method to the exigencies of the school situation.

But, while we would not wish to see the standard of performance in written work fall—it is low enough in many cases already—we may nevertheless need to adjust our thinking on the question of standards. If our objectives in language teaching have been somewhat altered, if our methods too are changing, if the new type of examinations are requiring a higher standard of oral production and less in the way of performance in the written language, then it is inevitable that adjustments need to be made in our view of standards. It is possible that the greatest intellectual challenge of the subject could lie in oral work; the demand for a certain level of accuracy and fluency in speech and in aural comprehension can stretch an able pupil every bit as much as the traditional requirements of written accuracy. What is involved is not so much a lowering of standards as a shift in emphasis. It could be that the new examinations were on the whole more difficult than the old ones, even though the same standard of written work were not required. As far as Ordinary level is concerned, however, any change in standard of written work is likely to be only small. If some pupils are to master the written language they must surely be among the Ordinary level candidates; in the C.S.E. examinations the case may be different. Whatever adjustments to standards may come we cannot allow a landslide. At the same time we must be receptive to a radically new conception of what proficiency in the use of language really is.

The New Examinations

These considerations bring us back to the question of examinations that we were considering in Chapter 7. Teachers in secondary schools are reasonably sure of the type of work that needs to be done at present to prepare pupils for Ordinary level examinations in modern languages. But if these examinations change in character, or if the C.S.E. becomes very widely accepted, what type of language teaching will be required in preparation for the new examinations? In many cases there will be no difficulty at all; many teachers work to a syllabus that includes such an important amount of oral work at all stages that the change could easily be made to an examination in which fifty per cent of the marks at least were given for oral aspects of the work.

In other cases there may be considerable difficulty. It is usual to give an important place to oral language work in the first two years of a secondary school course. The increasing use of audio-visual aids is simply serving to promote even more this oral work in the early years. The crucial difficulty is the continuation of this work beyond the second year. As adolescence comes upon the pupils they get more self-conscious and shy, less willing to express themselves spontaneously, and less willing to speak in a foreign language in front of their classmates. As the G.C.E. year approaches, the teacher is more and more anxious to provide for plenty of exercises of a written kind. In any case the pupils have now come up against some very real difficulties in the grammar of the language, and these seem to require treatment by studying rules and translating sentences. This situation is somewhat aggravated by the fact that many of the audio-visual courses do not provide for more than about two years' work. The problem then is how to maintain good oral work beyond the second year, and at the same time to provide for learning the written mode of the language. In order to prepare for the new types of examinations there must be a continual development of oral-aural skills in the third, fourth and fifth years, but at the same time the written language must be thoroughly learned.

It has been suggested that after an audio-visual course in the first two years there might well follow a stage in which the emphasis is mainly on comprehension. This would mean not only the comprehension of simple spoken dialogue, maintained from the audio-visual course, but also the comprehension of written texts. This comprehension stage might begin during the second year for the abler classes and would occupy the third year for most. For weaker pupils it might extend well into the fourth and fifth years. The visual element would not altogether be abandoned, but gradually, as is stated for the *Voix et Images* course, the sound would be liberated from the picture. Work would proceed on quite short narrative texts, specially chosen and suited lexically and grammatically to the knowledge of the pupils. Extensive use could be made of tape-recordings of such passages and abundant oral work, mainly of a question-and-answer kind could be based on them. The next step would be the use of readers for more extended reading of longer texts. The *Let's Read French* series of readers could be most valuable here in providing a transition from audio-visual teaching to extensive individual reading. A large number of readers of a more conventional kind are also available and as many as possible could be read by pupils at this stage.

In this comprehension stage, the study of grammar and work in written expression would not be altogether neglected. But a third stage of the course, in the fourth and fifth years, would be the time when considerably more emphasis would be placed on the skills of writing and on an understanding of the grammar of the written language. The comprehension stage should be an excellent preparation for this. Pupils would approach the study of grammar with considerable experience in reading and understanding the language. This third stage would be the preparation for examinations. With new types of examination in view it is clear that the aural-oral skills learned in the audio-visual stage must be maintained and constantly used and developed, while at the same time a start is made on the more formal study of the grammar of the written language.

Schools that are fortunate enough to have a language laboratory may well find that the skilful use of this equipment goes a long way towards keeping the study of the oral language alive. There could be satisfactory links between the oral drills of the laboratory and the work on the written language. Some of the techniques of the laboratory might well be transferred to the classroom for the development of pattern practice. In any case the impetus to oral work provided by French in the primary school, and by the use of audio-visual aids, will need to be kept going. The formation of right attitudes and right habits of language learning in the early years will do much to help later on. When the examinations change, the final years of the Ordinary level course will be bound to change too. The predominance of written translation work will have to yield to oral activities, conversation work, reading aloud, and so on. Gradually, we may hope, a new pattern of teaching languages should establish itself in secondary schools, according to which pupils will be taught the spoken language as well as the elements of the written language, and will be taught by means of oral practice.

Literature and the Sixth Form

The swing towards teaching languages as communication has made people think that this is to the detriment of the study of literature. The suggestions now being put forward that there should be non-literary language courses in the sixth form seem to have justified these fears. But there are other considerations which may be very favourable to the reading of literature. The earlier start on language learning and the use of audio-visual methods will mean that at an earlier age than previously pupils will have the ability to approach the reading of contemporary literary texts. It may well be that in the fourth and fifth years of grammar schools pupils will be able to read straightforward narrative texts—short stories, novels, biography and travel. There can be no question at this stage of systematic study of the more difficult philosophical questions that literature entails, nor of embarking on texts, such as seventeenth century French tragedy, that often need to be situated historically to be understood. It will be a case of rapid reading for enjoyment. The objective will be that at this age the abler pupils may read a little in a foreign literature that is comparable to the type of book that they may be expected to read in their mother tongue. There could well be a progression from readers of the kind now being produced in the *Let's Read French* series to simple stories by Simenon and then to selected works of Daninos, Maupassant, Frison-Roche, St-Exupéry, Duhamel, Troyat and many others whose short stories and novels appear in English editions. This reading would not be limited to *belles lettres,* but would include books of travel and adventure that would interest young people and give them a wide acquaintance with French life and achievement. The lists suggested in *Modern Languages in the Grammar School* give many examples of books of this kind.[1] Not all pupils, even in a selected stream would be able to manage such a programme, but sufficient reading could be done in class for pupils to be set in the right direction and some of the abler ones could go further on their own.

Middle school reading of this kind would not be intended necessarily to lead to literary studies in the sixth form. There will probably always be a few specialists taking a modern languages course to Advanced level in which the study of literature has a most important place. But far too often in our grammar schools the reading of foreign literature has been the preserve of this select group. There are now possibilities of more pupils being able to sample some of the works of modern foreign writers, even though they may have no thought of following a literary course.

If we are to provide adequately for the needs of our day we must also plan non-literary language courses in the sixth form. These will not be simply a minority course for specialists in some other subject, though courses of this kind may still

---

[1] I.A.H.M. (Division 12), *Modern Languages in the Grammar School,* rev. ed., 1966. Appendix B, pp. 55-68 and Appendix F, pp. 79-82.

be needed too. But it will be necessary to develop courses which provide for a major part of a pupil's work to Advanced level. It might be possible, for example, to take two sciences and a language, or history, economics and a language, and in each case the course would not have a major literary element. The spoken and written language would be studied to a standard beyond that normally reached at Advanced level. At the same time the course would include some social studies of the country concerned in geography, history, economics or the arts. This could lead to the new type of Advanced level examination that we mentioned in Chapter 7

Some Other Possibilities

The authors of the Annan Report, *The Teaching of Russian,* suggested that 'the scope of modern language teaching in secondary schools might well be broadened if the regular teaching of a first modern language were started in good conditions and by the right methods in primary schools to pupils aged nine years who would be able to continue that language in their secondary schools and spend fewer periods on it, thus making time for a second language'.[1] They envisaged that the first language in such a case would be French and that the second might well be Russian. The idea put forward here suggests a new approach to an old problem. It was at the end of World War II that Allison Peers made a vigorous attack on the 'French monopoly', by which he meant the strong position of French as the first foreign language to be taught in this country's schools[2]. However good and just may be the claims of French to be the principal foreign language taught in our schools, it is undeniable that the amount of French teaching that takes place, compared with the amount of German, Spanish or Russian teaching, is out of all proportion to the relative importance of French. The Norwood Report recommended that French and German should be alternatives

[1] *The Teaching of Russian* (Annan Report), H.M.S.O., 1962, p. 21.
[2] E. A. Peers, *"New" Tongues or Modern Language Teaching of the Future,* Pitman, 1945. See especially Chapter 3.

more often than is the practice in schools, and that Spanish should become the chief language in some schools, and particularly in areas which have ties with Spanish-speaking countries[1]. The Ministry of Education's pamphlet on Modern Languages stated cheerfully in 1956 that some of the Norwood recommendations had borne fruit[2]. This was true, but it could hardly be said at that time that there was adequate variety in the languages taught or adequate importance given to Spanish, Russian or Italian. The Annan committee did at least glimpse a possible means of giving substantially more importance in our schools to languages other than French.

Of recent years the problem of a diversity of languages has become even more acute. We can no longer afford to be complacent about the 'French monopoly'. The Annan Report made clear what is the desperate position of Russian teaching in this country. Even now far too little is being done to promote the teaching of Russian in schools. There are cases of graduate teachers in our schools who are qualified to teach Russian, but who are not being allowed to teach the language because the head of the school is afraid that in a year or two the teacher concerned will leave for promotion and that it will not be possible to appoint another teacher of Russian. Russian teaching in the school would then abruptly end. But before we have solved the problem of the supply of teachers of Russian, we have further problems on our hands. Chinese is now a world language and Arabic is increasing in importance as the Arab bloc becomes a more and more influential factor in the world. Not only are these two great languages now able to claim some recognition at least in our schools, but others such as Swahili and Urdu are following hard behind them.

The first step towards facing these problems is probably to improve the quality of language teaching as it is in our schools. All that we have been considering in this book has this objective. When a first modern language is widely taught in primary schools, when audio-visual aids are extensively and

[1] *Curriculum and Examinations in Secondary Schools* (Norwood Report), H.M.S.O., 1943, p. 117.

[2] Ministry of Education pamphlet no. 29, *Modern Languages*, H.M.S.O., 1956, p. 17.

successfully employed, when language laboratories are available in nearly all senior comprehensive and grammar schools, then we may be in a position so to organise language teaching that a more adequate place is found for Russian and Spanish, and probably for other languages as well. Pupils who have been taught French by active oral methods in the primary school will not be daunted by the prospect of another language to be learned at a later stage. The Annan committee's suggestion certainly deserves to be followed up.

In some schools experiments have been made in using a foreign language as the medium of instruction in some other subjects in the curriculum. This has been done at both primary and secondary levels. In one large comprehensive school a group of eleven-year-old pupils of less than grammar-school ability were given a timetable in which just over half the periods were devoted to French. After a period of intensive language learning for the first few weeks of the year, the time available for French was used for teaching science, history, geography, some mathematics, physical education and drama, using French as the medium of instruction. It was found at the end of the year that the group had done as well in the subjects taught in French as had a control group, who had been taught in the mother tongue. The experimental class were of course greatly superior to the control group in oral-aural performance in the foreign language, and were slightly better in achievement in the written language.

This can be regarded as no more than an interesting experiment, but an experiment that could no doubt be repeated with profit in various schools. It would probably not become part of the regular pattern of language teaching, but we should be open to the possibility of such projects being arranged as and when it may be thought suitable. Such a project could be followed up by certain pupils spending a term or a year in a school in France. The benefit to be gained from such an experience is self-evident as far as language learning is concerned. Problems of arranging an exchange of pupils, even on a limited scale, between two schools in different countries are very considerable. The parents' views and wishes must be a deciding factor in any case. We must however be ready for such diversity in our language teaching that valuable projects of this kind are possible and welcomed by language teachers, who would need to do a great deal of work to provide for the pupils the fullest advantage that can be gained from such experiences.

The Future Pattern

We can now summarise this chapter by tracing the main features of the new pattern of language teaching in secondary schools. There will be much diversity and variation. But no longer will the experience of language learning be the privilege of the few; it will be available to all, or nearly all. Second, foreign language teaching will not start in the secondary school in most cases, and therefore close links will have to be maintained with the teachers in primary schools. Third, methods of teaching will take full advantage of audio-visual aids, and, in the later years, of language laboratories, whenever this is possible. Fourth, the main emphasis will be on the spoken language, and this will be evident both in teaching methods and in examining techniques. This does not mean that the written language or its literature will be neglected, particularly in the case of the more able pupils. Finally, we can expect that the range of languages taught in our schools will increase and the possibilities of teaching languages such as Russian, Spanish and others, will be exploited more fully than at present.

The most significant change that we are looking for is not, however, simply an organisational one. It is a change in our national attitude to language learning. It is to be hoped that all these developments will help us to realise as a nation how vital language learning is. We must come to accept as a normal element in our national life that everybody will learn something of at least one foreign language, and that anybody, if called upon to do so, could reach a reasonable degree of proficiency in the oral use of that language for communication, according to his own personal ability and needs.

Further Education and the Training of Teachers

This book is mainly about language teaching in schools. But to complete the account of the new pattern something must be said about language teaching in education beyond school. It is not intended to give a full description of developments in technical colleges, colleges of education and universities, but simply to pick out the principal features of language teaching in these institutions that are having a noticeable effect on the schools. In the first place, technical colleges have led the way in the development of new techniques of language teaching and in the use of language laboratories. We must therefore refer more explicitly to what they have done. Second, the training of the language teacher of the future may in some cases be significantly different from the training such teachers have received in the past. This again will be important for the schools in which they will teach.

Technical Colleges

While the work in Colleges of Advanced Technology is best considered later, along with university work, language teaching in Regional, Area and Local Colleges is taken together in this section. There may of course be great differences between the work in one of these three types of colleges and that in another. At the most elementary level there are classes in which the conversational language is taught to adults who wish to travel for holidays and tourism. There are also courses leading to Ordinary and Advanced level of G.C.E., or to the Ordinary

National and Higher National Certificates and Diplomas, and these are often provided for young people on day-release from industry or commerce. One or more languages may figure in courses in business studies, in secretarial courses or in other professional courses. There has been a tremendous increase of recent years in the demand for language courses for salesmen, scientists, technologists, company directors or other executives in industry and business. These men and women need to acquire the ability to use a spoken language for the purpose of conducting business abroad, attending board meetings of international companies, or for some other work in their business life. We noticed in Chapter 2 how the F.B.I. has emphasised in two reports[1] that there is a great need for staff at all levels who have a working knowledge of a foreign language, and who are able to communicate uninhibitedly in that language. Generally speaking the need is for ability in the spoken language. Fluency is considered more important than perfect pronunciation, and the capacity to understand and to express oneself is preferred to grammatical accuracy.

Often these students require to learn a language quickly in a limited space of time. They may have only a few months available before an important foreign business meeting. They may sometimes be prepared in the period available to devote most of their time to learning the language in question. In this way crash courses have been arranged in some colleges, or sometimes by certain commercial undertakings. Such courses serve the purpose of teaching a language in a limited time, and, like the ASTP programme in America, they have achieved remarkable success. Whatever doubts we might entertain about the educational value of this type of teaching, crash courses continue to be widely used and have been found effective within their limited training objectives. For the adult learner there needs to be a large allocation of time for efficient language learning. A course which involves several hours per day seems to be appropriate for adult learning, even though it might be impossible for the younger learner in school. We must remember, however, that in the repetitive drills of oral

[1] See pp. 29-31.

language learning there is a point beyond which the brain begins to flag, and the student may continue to repeat, but without full understanding and without real learning taking place. In organising a crash course care must be taken to avoid this kind of fatigue.

In the larger colleges that have departments solely or mainly concerned with modern languages, a wide range of courses in various languages is available. At Holborn College of Law, Languages and Commerce, for example, courses are offered in more than twenty languages ranging from Portuguese to Serbo-Croat and from Afrikaans to Yoruba, and including most of the major tongues of Europe, Asia and Africa. At some of the provincial colleges, such as the Liverpool or Birmingham Colleges of Commerce a very good selection of languages is also available, related more to regional needs. In most areas local demands for full-time or part-time courses in French, German, Italian, Spanish or Russian can be met by the local colleges. In some cases more specialised needs are also met locally; Grimsby College of Further Education provides courses in Danish, while in Bradford, where there is a considerable immigrant population, courses in Urdu are available at the Technical College. The Ministry of Education's circular 2/64 of 2 March 1964[1] approved this general pattern, and encouraged colleges to cooperate with local industry in providing the courses required. In the case of some of the rarer languages the Minister suggested that courses should be provided at a limited number of centres only, according to regional and national needs.

It is in technical colleges that new techniques of language teaching have been developed in this country of recent years. The first language laboratory to be provided in Britain by an education authority was installed in Ealing Technical College in 1961, and it was there under the direction of Miss Mabel Sculthorp, Head of the Department of General Studies, that much pioneering work was done in laboratory teaching methods and in the development of courses. Many other

[1] Quoted in full in F.B.I. working party report, *Foreign Language Needs of Industry*, 1964, pp. 45-49.

colleges soon followed Ealing in using both language laboratories and audio-visual courses. The first book to be published about language laboratories on the basis of experience in Britain was the work of two teachers at the City of Westminster College, and appeared in 1963. In most cases it has been found necessary in the colleges to produce the programmes needed for use in the laboratories. This has involved a great deal of work for the teachers in analysing the linguistic material to be presented, preparing the exercises and making the recordings. The leading example of this is found in the excellent courses in German and Spanish that have been produced at Ealing Technical College. These courses, arranged in carefully graded lesson units, are specially orientated towards the needs of commerce. Most of the work at Ealing has been done in crash courses for business executives, and it has been found that language laboratory courses provide the most effective means of conducting such courses. In each unit of one of the Ealing courses linguistic material is presented in dialogue form and then is developed by means of structure drills and other exercises. The National Committee for Audio-visual Aids in Education found that in the sector of technical education there was considerably more satisfaction with achievements in language laboratory teaching than there was in secondary schools[1]. More mature students with clear motivation seem to be better able to profit from this type of work.

University Degree Courses

The undergraduate modern languages courses that have been established in our universities since the latter part of the last century have, until recently, followed a similar pattern everywhere, with some variations. The staple diet of the courses has been language and literature. The language element usually consists of translation work from and into the modern language, with a strong bias towards the language of literature, some essay work, the development of conversational

[1] National Committee for Audio-Visual Aids in Education, *The Use of Language Laboratories in Great Britain*, 1965, p. 15.

proficiency in the spoken language, and philology or the historical study of the development of the language. The work on literature involves a study of literature from medieval times to the present day, with emphasis, sometimes by students' choice, on certain significant periods or authors. In German the works of Goethe and his contemporaries, in French the literature of the seventeenth century, and in Spanish the works of the Golden Age, are all likely to figure importantly in undergraduate studies. Contemporary literature is usually included, but may or may not receive very much attention. It is therefore not unusual for a student to spend most of his time on the study of medieval language and literature and in the study of literature before the twentieth century. It must be added, however, that a period of residence in the foreign country is usually an essential part of the course, that some study is often made of the life and institutions of the country, and that real proficiency in the use of the spoken language is achieved by the majority of students[1].

These courses do not aim to provide professional training for language teachers, interpreters or others. They seek rather to provide a truly humane education through linguistic and literary studies. The academic quality and the educational value of these courses is widely recognised, and graduates from university language departments have proved their worth in many walks of life. There have been many adjustments and minor variations introduced into these courses, which may be taken in one language only, or in two. At times emphasis may be placed on contemporary literature rather than on philology, or literary studies may be linked with an interest in history, philosophy or the social sciences. Combined honours courses have also linked a modern language with another arts subject, such as English or history, as twin components of a degree course. Over the years increased attention has been given to the command of the language in speech and writing, and there

[1] For full details of the courses see H. H. Stern, ed., *Modern Languages in the Universities (A Guide to Courses)*. 2nd edn. Macmillan, 1965. See also two articles by Stern in *Modern Languages,* Vol. XLV, Nos. 2 and 3, June and September 1964; and E. Koutaissoff, 'New Trends in Modern Language Studies' in *Modern Languages,* Vol. XLVI, No. 3, September 1965.

has been a more enlightened approach to the study of literature.

In the new universities which are now being established, and in the Colleges of Advanced Technology which are to become universities, new types of modern languages courses are being set up, which do not merely show changes of emphasis within a traditional framework, but which differ fundamentally from the linguistic-literary studies. Some of these newer courses regard modern languages as part of purely contemporary studies; work on the medieval language and literature is dispensed with, and attention is concentrated on the language as it is today and on the literature, history, economics, sociology, politics or geography of countries where the language is spoken. The Universities of Sussex and East Anglia have each a School of European Studies in which students study the civilisation of Europe through language and literature seen against a background of philosophy and the social sciences. The University of Essex has a School of Comparative Studies which offers schemes of study either in government or in literature; the Language Centre of that university provides intensive language courses in support of the comparative studies and also concentrates on general and applied linguistics, which help to unite the study of several languages. The Department of Language in the University of York offers courses not only in European languages, but also in Hindi, Pali, Sanskrit, Sinhalese, Yoruba, Swahili; and it is hoped soon to add Tamil, Malay and Chinese to this list. Considerable emphasis is placed on linguistics, and a non-European language can be combined with another subject as suitable preparation for teaching or diplomatic work in Commonwealth countries.

In the Colleges of Advanced Technology, some of which have now achieved university status, there are courses which have clearly vocational orientation, and which sometimes link language study with business studies, science and technology. The new University of Bradford has a four-year course of applied Language Studies to be taken in at least two languages. Studies include literature, thought, social sciences, and the history of science and technology. The third year is spent abroad, sometimes with an industrial firm, and during this time students are required to prepare a dissertation on some social, economic or linguistic aspect of life in the foreign country. The fourth year includes practice in simultaneous interpreting as well as studies of international affairs. In the University of Strathclyde a modern language can be combined with business economics, commerce, marketing, accountancy, secretarial practice or human relations; in such a course the modern language component includes both language and linguistics on the one hand, and also literature and civilisation on the other.

Language departments in the older 'redbrick' universities may be influenced to some extent by these new developments. But it is not to be expected that the traditional linguistic–literary degree courses will suffer a decline. They are too valuable and too well established. They may however be modified in some cases, or alternative courses may grow up alongside them. In any case the new types of courses, have to prove themselves and to gain recognition. As far as schools are concerned these developments are significant in two ways. First, a number of modern linguists will go on from sixth forms to new types of language degree courses, and these pupils may not be primarily interested in literature. This may open the way for alternatives to literary studies in sixth-form modern language courses. Second, some of the graduates of the newer universities will return to schools to teach. They will bring with them a fresh approach to language teaching, maybe a considerable knowledge of linguistics and an interest in the applications of language in technology, commerce and the social sciences. Such teachers could be most valuable in certain schools and in certain areas.

Training Graduate Teachers

Graduates who intend to take up teaching as a career are usually trained for their professional work in university departments of education. The course normally includes study of various aspects of education—theory, history, psychology etc.—and is of one year's duration, leading to a diploma or graduate certificate in education. Some colleges of education also run a one-year course for graduates, which is very similar to the course in a university. It is during this year in a university department or a college of education that the modern languages graduate receives instruction in how to teach his subject.

Traditionally this instruction is given by means of a 'method course', that is a course of lectures or classes on the philosophy of the subject, on the principles underlying its teaching and on the method by which it should be presented in the classroom. As far as possible the method course is linked with the student's own experience on teaching practice in schools, of which he is required to do a number of weeks in the course of the year. In various subjects, including modern languages, it is now found for a variety of reasons that the method course alone is not enough to equip the teacher for work in the classroom. Teaching today often involves the use of mechanical aids and equipment, and the teacher in training needs some instruction, not only in the physical manipulation of such aids, but also in methods by which the use of these aids is to be suitably integrated into a well designed lesson. The scientist needs help in conducting work in the laboratory, the geographer needs to learn what use can be made of visual aids such as films and slides, and the modern linguist has to learn how to use tape-recorder and film-strip projector in an audiovisual lesson and how to run a language laboratory. There are two aspects of this work; the first is the learning of how to operate the equipment—a purely practical matter—and the second is the pedagogical question of how to use the equipment to the best advantage in the teaching situation. Clearly to do this adequately a department of education needs to have the right equipment available, but many departments have no language laboratory. Also a generous amount of time is necessary if each student is to gain some experience in using the equipment. As more and more schools use audio-visual aids and language laboratories, students have more opportunities of using them on teaching practice, but still they need to have some knowledge of the appropriate techniques before they go to the schools. We can also hope that within a few years every modern languages graduate will have had extensive experience of a language laboratory in his undergraduate course.

A second difficulty confronting the method lecturer springs from the very nature of these undergraduate courses. Having been steeped for several years in the literary traditions and translation disciplines of sixth forms and university language departments, the young graduate finds it difficult, unless he was exceptionally well taught at school, to envisage a kind of language teaching that is primarily oral and that is concerned with the spoken rather than the written language. Indeed, he may not have a very clear theoretical conception of what language is and how it operates. It is perfectly possible to learn to speak a language excellently, as indeed most modern languages honours graduates can, but yet have the most erroneous ideas about language on the theoretical level or about how language is most efficiently learned. At least one department of education has been obliged to run a course on linguistics for modern linguists, classicists and English specialists.

More effective work can be done in training the language teacher by means of practical work. Even a simple visit to a primary school where a foreign language is being taught, has succeeded far better in convincing many students about the possibilities of teaching the spoken language than a whole series of method lectures could ever hope to. But better than this is some experience for the students in the learning situation. Ideally the language teacher in training should relive the language learning experience by being taught a totally unfamiliar language by oral methods. It is sometimes possible for one student who has a knowledge of, say, Russian or modern Greek, to teach this language to a group of his fellow students in a language laboratory. The experience makes all concerned think more deeply than ever about the true nature of language learning.

There is another problem in the training of graduate

teachers today. Formerly departments of education could safely regard themselves as the training ground for the academic specialist who was to teach in a grammar school. With the changes that have already come about in the organisation of education this limited view of the department's function is no longer possible. Some students go out to teach the eleven to thirteen age range in junior high schools, some teach only the thirteen-plus pupils in senior high schools, some specialise on the lower streams of comprehensive schools, while others may go into sixth-form colleges or even into further education. It may be possible in some departments of education to direct certain courses towards certain levels of teaching, or to allow students options according to the type of teaching in which they are interested. The modern languages method course, however, though it may be subdivided into a French course, a German course and a Russian course, can rarely, if ever, be further fragmented according to various levels of teaching. The method lecturer has a considerable variety of future teachers in his class. He has to frame his course as broadly as possible to include them all.

Colleges of Education

In the old pattern of language teaching that has existed up to the 1960s, it has been normal for teachers of modern languages to be graduates. Their training has generally consisted of a university degree course, often a year in the foreign country, and the year's work in a department of education, which we have just been considering. Such a training, lasting five years at least, is thoroughly sound and there is no reason to mistrust the principles on which it is based. There may be modifications and improvements to be made; changes may come, as we have seen, in the nature of the degree course; the year of professional training may soon be made compulsory, and some would like to see it extended; but basically university study, foreign residence and professional training are the essential elements in the preparation of the academic languages teacher.

The extension of language teaching to the full ability range in comprehensive schools and to the younger age groups in primary schools means that in the future language teaching in British schools will not be solely in the hands of graduates. It is unlikely that there would ever be enough modern languages graduates entering teaching to provide for this great extension of language teaching. Graduates are often not particularly suited by ability, inclination or training for teaching younger children, or perhaps one should say that their ability is better used with the older and more able pupils. This is not to suggest that the teaching of young children or children of less than average ability is easier, or that it requires less ability on the part of the teacher. Indeed the contrary may be true. But the fact is that primary schools are mainly staffed by non-graduates, and in most comprehensive schools less than half the teachers are university trained. It is inevitable then that a large proportion of language teaching in this country will be done by teachers who have been trained in colleges of education. Some of these will be graduates, when arrangements for the new B.Ed. degree are under way. The Modern Language Association already includes in its membership a number of primary school teachers, and this trend towards a removal of the barriers within the teaching body can do much to help towards a unifying of the profession.

In the past only very few training colleges have offered French as a main subject, but now a very great interest in languages has arisen in the colleges. Many colleges of education are building up modern languages departments and providing courses in French, and in some cases in other languages as well. It is interesting to notice what the nature of these three-year courses is. While there is a tendency to be influenced by university degree courses, the colleges have a large amount of freedom in shaping their own syllabuses, and are doing so with the practical needs of the teacher in mind. The courses are not only a preparation for teaching, but are also intended for the personal development of the individual. It must be remembered that a student who is following a main course in French may also be following a main course in another subject. He will also be studying various branches of education, and devoting some of his time to English and also to some 'curriculum subjects'.

Main courses in modern languages usually place very considerable emphasis on the spoken language and on proficiency in its use. A number of colleges have installed language laboratories and use these extensively to develop the students' command of the spoken language. The study of literary texts forms an important part of the work. Selected works from a representative range of authors are studied in some detail, and there is some concentration on twentieth century writers. Models of the written language for study and possible translation are taken not only from literary works, but also from newspapers, magazines, autobiography, travel books, and so on. It is usually arranged for students to spend a period abroad, either in a teacher training establishment in the foreign country, or in attendance at a university vacation course. Attention is given to the life and civilisation of the foreign people, and the student may be required to make an area study of a part of the foreign country he has visited. Colleges are also showing interest in general linguistics as a basic element in the training of the languages teacher. The course always includes the methodology of teaching languages, and here the use of audio-visual courses has an important place. There is of course a great deal of variety from college to college; all we can do here is to pick out some of the salient features which frequently arise. In general, however, such courses are practically based in the spoken language and in a study of the contemporary culture of the foreign nation.

A small number of the most able students will continue their studies for a fourth year to take a B.Ed. degree at the university in their area. Courses of study for this will again vary a good deal in different parts of the country. In any case the degree itself will be a degree in education, as the Robbins report recommended[1]. But there may be a study of the academic subject as a component in the degree, or the student might do much of his work for the degree in the areas of linguistics or methodology. This will mean that there will be a few

[1] *Higher Education* (Robbins Report), H.M.S.O., 1963, para. 341.

graduate language teachers entering the schools who have done considerably more work in these areas than many teachers who have taken an honours degree in modern languages and done a year's professional training. This development is likely to bring enrichment into the language teaching profession. College trained teachers, whether graduates or not, will have a valuable contribution to make to the teaching of languages in our schools.

Conclusion

The various changes in language teaching in Britain that have been considered in this book are not to be regarded as isolated developments. All that we have considered is linked together in one great forward movement in language teaching. Basic to this movement is the development of the ideas about language and language teaching which we surveyed in Part One. Perhaps the most important aspect of these ideas has been the growing realisation of the importance of speech. From this has emerged the notion of teaching languages primarily as a means of oral communication and also a clearer understanding of the vital role of speech in the language learning process.

The growth of these ideas has on the one hand paved the way for the developments in teaching and testing techniques which we considered in Part Two. On the other hand the availability of audio-visual courses, television and language laboratories has greatly helped forward the newer ideas on language teaching and on the importance of speech. Not all the developments we mentioned in Part Two are of equal importance. Probably the use of audio-visual courses is the most significant factor here, as far as schools are concerned, closely followed by the growth of language laboratories. There are other developments in teaching techniques, such as the use of programmed learning, the true value of which it is still very difficult to assess for language teaching.

When in Part Three we came to consider the effects of these ideas and techniques in practice in the schools, we had to relate language teaching to changes which are at present taking place in the school system of Britain and in the curriculum within the schools. In the new comprehensive education a modern foreign language may be taught to almost all pupils, of whatever type of ability and of whatever social background they may be. This may prove to be the greatest single change in language teaching in our schools. Current developments in teaching method and in the use of audio-visual aids bring this extension of language teaching much more within the bounds of possibility than ever before. At the same time languages are being taught in primary schools and are far more important in further education than was the case some years ago. The place of languages in higher education is in some institutions taking on a new aspect.

All these developments are to be seen as one whole, and as linked with the social, economic and educational trends of our times. We cannot arrest the forces at work, nor can we put the clock back. A new pattern of language teaching is taking shape in our schools. All language teachers and others concerned with language teaching need to become familiar with the new pattern. Some traditional notions will have to be rejected: language teaching is not the preserve of selective secondary schools, nor is it essentially linked with the study of literature, nor is it necessarily a training in precision of written expression. Language teaching in the new pattern will be available to all and will be mainly concerned with communication in speech, an essential element in various branches of education. New techniques will not necessarily bring a miraculous improvement in the teaching and learning of languages; we must not expect to make linguists of all people in Britain. But language teaching can become vastly more efficient and at the same time provide a truly human element in the education of large numbers of pupils and students.

Bibliography

This list of books on language teaching is intended to be practical. It is by no means exhaustive, and indeed if it had been it would have been too vast to be useful. The aim has been to mention all those books, available in Britain, which seem to me to be of major significance, and a number of others which, while not perhaps of major significance, provide valuable reading. No attempt has been made to list all the books and articles referred to in the course of this book. But the teacher or the teacher in training will find here a selection of reading in which he can broaden and deepen his knowledge of language teaching in whatever direction he wishes. Bibliographies given in some of the works listed here will carry the reader even further.

For convenience the list is divided into sections. The first section, 'General A', contains books about language teaching in general which appeared before about 1960, and therefore do not include references to new developments such as language laboratories. Section 'General B' contains books on language teaching in general which have appeared recently and are specifically concerned with recent developments. This is perhaps the most important section of the bibliography and all the books listed in it are vital reading. The section on 'Linguistics' is intentionally limited and contains mainly books on linguistics applied to language teaching. In the book by Robins and in the one by Halliday, McIntosh and Strevens, there are excellent bibliographies to which the reader interested in wider aspects of linguistics is advised to turn.

Professor Mackey's book gives an almost exhaustive analysis of the problems of language teaching and contains the largest bibliography of the subject available anywhere. Audio-visual aids and language laboratories are grouped together in the next section simply because a number of books deal with both. Some books in section 2 could equally well have been placed in this section. Books on primary school work and on examining are given in sections 5 and 6. In section 7 a few books are given which do not conveniently fit into the other categories. Finally, the most useful periodicals devoted wholly or mainly to language teaching are listed in the last section.

1 *General, A*

CLOSSET, F. R. *Didactique des Langues Vivantes.* Brussels and Paris: Didier, 3rd edn, 1956. 252 pp.

COULSON, E. L. *French in the Secondary School.* Edinburgh: Nelson, 1947. viii, 159 pp.

HODGSON, F. M. *Learning Modern Languages.* London: Routledge and Kegan Paul, 1955. ix, 100 pp.

HUEBENER, T. *How to Teach Foreign Languages Effectively.* New York: University Press, 1960. x, 198 pp.

INCORPORATED ASSOCIATION OF ASSISTANT MASTERS. *The Teaching of Modern Languages.* London: University of London Press, 3rd edn, 1956. 343 pp.

JESPERSON, O. *How to Teach a Foreign Language.* London: Allen and Unwin, 1904, reprinted 1956. 194 pp.

MALLINSON, V. *Teaching a Modern Language.* London: Heinemann, 1953. 135 pp.

MINISTRY OF EDUCATION. *Modern Languages* (Pamphlet No. 29). London: H.M.S.O., 1956. vii, 111 pp.

PEERS, E. A. *"New" Tongues.* London: Pitman, 1945. 151 pp.

THIMANN, I. C. *Teaching Languages*. London: Harrap, 1955. 151 pp.

UNESCO. *The Teaching of Modern Languages: a volume of studies*. Paris: UNESCO, 1955. 295 pp.

2 *General, B*

BELYAYEV, B. V. *The Psychology of Teaching Foreign Languages*. Oxford: Pergamon Press, 1963, ix, 230 pp.

CALVERT, F. I. *French by Modern Methods in Primary and Secondary Schools*. Huddersfield: Schofield and Sims, 1965. 96 pp.

DUTTON, B., ed. *A Guide to Modern Language Teaching Methods*. AVLA Publication No. 1. London: Cassell, 1965. 206 pp.

INCORPORATED ASSOCIATION OF HEADMASTERS: *Modern Languages in the Grammar School*. Report of a working party set up by Division 12 (Lancashire and Cheshire). London: I.A.H.M., rev. edn, 1966. 93 pp.

JAMES, C. V., ed. *On Teaching Russian*. Oxford: Pergamon Press, 1963. xi, 143 pp.

LADO, R. *Language Teaching: A Scientific Approach*. New York: McGraw-Hill, 1964. xiv, 239 pp.

LIBBISH, B., ed. *Advances in the Teaching of Modern Languages*. Oxford: Pergamon Press, 1963. ix, 175 pp.

RIVERS, W. M. *The Psychologist and the Foreign Language Teacher*. Chicago: The University of Chicago Press, 1964. viii, 212 pp.

Various Authors: *New Research and Techniques for the Benefit of Modern Language Teaching*. Strasbourg: Council for Cultural Co-operation of the Council of Europe, 1964. 187 pp.

Various Authors: *Recent Developments in Modern Language Teaching*. Strasbourg: Council for Cultural Co-operation of the Council of Europe, 1964. 43 pp.

3 *Linguistics*

ABERCROMBIE, D. *Problems and Principles*. London: Longmans, 1956. vi, 97 pp.

CARROLL, J. B. *The Study of Language*. Cambridge, U.S.A., Harvard University Press, 1953. xi, 289 pp.

ENKVIST, N. E., SPENCER, J., and GREGORY, M. J. *Linguistics and Style*. London: Oxford University Press, 1964. xii, 109 pp.

HALLIDAY, M. A. K., MᶜINTOSH, A., and STREVENS, P. *The Linguistic Sciences and Language Teaching*. London: Longmans, 1964. xix, 322 pp.

MACKEY, W. F. *Language Teaching Analysis*. London: Longmans, 1965. xi, 554 pp.

POLITZER, R. L. *Teaching French: An Introduction to Applied Linguistics*. London: Ginn, 1960. iv, 140 pp.

ROBINS, R. H. *General Linguistics: An Introductory Survey*. London: Longmans, 1964. xxii, 390 pp.

4 *Audio-Visual Aids and Language Laboratories*

ADAM, J. B. and SHAWCROSS, A. J. *The Language Laboratory*. London: Pitman, 1963. viii, 72 pp

CORDER, S. P. *The Visual Element in Language Teaching*. London: Longmans, 1966. xi, 96 pp.

HICKEL, R. *Modern Language Teaching by Television*. Strasbourg: Council for Cultural Co-operation of the Council of Europe, 1965. 185 pp.

HILTON, J. B. *The Language Laboratory in School*. London: Methuen, 1964. 150 pp.

MARTY, F. L. *Language Laboratory Learning*. Wellesley, Mass.: Audio-Visual Publications, 1960. 255 pp.

MARTY, F. L. *Programming a Basic Foreign Languages Course: Prospects for Self-instruction*. Hollin's College, Virginia, 1962. 69 pp.

NUFFIELD FOREIGN LANGUAGE TEACHING MATERIALS PROJECT. *Audio-Visual French Courses for Primary Schools—An Annotated Bibliography*. London: The Nuffield Foundation, 1965. 70 pp.

STACK, E. M. *The Language Laboratory and Modern Language Teaching*. New York: Oxford University Press, 1960. 149 pp.

TURNER, J. D. *Introduction to the Language Laboratory*. London: University of London Press, 1965. 110 pp.

VERNON, P. J. *The Use of Language Laboratories in Great Britain*. London: National Committee for Audio-Visual Aids in Education, 1965. 31 pp.

VERNON, P. J., ed. *The Audio-Visual Approach to Modern Language Teaching—a symposium*. London: National Committee for Audio-Visual Aids in Education, 1965. 72 pp.

5 *Language Teaching in Primary Schools*

ANDERSSON, T. *The Teaching of Foreign Languages in the Elementary School*. Boston: Heath and Co., 1953. 119 pp.

COLE, L. R. *Teaching French to Juniors*. London: University of London Press, 1964. 96 pp.

DUNKEL, H. B. and PILLET, R. A. *French in the Elementary School*. Chicago: University of Chicago Press, 1962. 150 pp.

KELLERMANN, M. *Two Experiments on Language Teaching in Primary Schools in Leeds*. London: Nuffield Foundation, 1964. vii, 77 pp.

LAZARO, C. M. *Report on Foreign Language Teaching in British Primary Schools, January–March* 1963. Leeds: The Nuffield Foundation Foreign Languages Teaching Materials Project, 1963. 21 pp. Mimeographed.

STERN, H. H. *Foreign Languages in Primary Education*. Hamburg: Unesco Institute for Education, 1963. 103 pp.

THOMAS, F. G. and LEACH, P. *Introducing French in a Primary School*. London: Macmillan, 1965. 58 pp.

6 *Examinations*

LADO, R. *Language Testing*. London: Longmans, 1961. 389 pp.

MANCHESTER SCHOOL OF EDUCATION C.S.E. RESEARCH PROJECT. *Interim Report of Modern Languages Panel*. Manchester School of Education, 1965.

OTTER, H. S. *Report, 1963-1966, of Modern Languages Association Examinations Project*. Institute of Education, University of Leeds, 1966. 96 + 40 pp. Mimeographed.

7 *Other Aspects of Language Teaching*

ANNAN COMMITTEE. *The Teaching of Russian*. Report of the Committee appointed by the Minister of Education and the Secretary of State for Scotland in September, 1960. London: H.M.S.O., 1960. v, 55 pp.

DODSON, C. J. *The Bilingual Method*. Aberystwyth: Faculty of Education, University College of Wales, 1962. 39 pp.

FEDERATION OF BRITISH INDUSTRIES. *Foreign Languages in Industry*. Report of a Working Party. London: F.B.I., 1962. vi, 49 pp.

FEDERATION OF BRITISH INDUSTRIES. *Foreign Language Needs of Industry*. Report of a Working Party. London: F.B.I., 1964. iv. 80 pp.

KREUSLER, A. *The Teaching of Modern Languages in the Soviet Union*. Leiden: E. J. Brill, 1963. 129 pp.

LEATHES COMMITTEE. *Modern Studies*. Report of the committee on the position of modern languages in the educational system of Great Britain. London: H.M.S.O., 1918, reprinted 1928. xxvi, 262 pp.

LOWE, M. and LOWE, J., eds. *On Teaching Foreign Languages to Adults: A Symposium*. Oxford: Pergamon Press, 1965. 152 pp.

MODERN LANGUAGES ASSOCIATION. *Modern Languages in the Sixth Form*. Report of a Committee. London: M.L.A., 1960. 59 pp.

MODERN LANGUAGES ASSOCIATION. *Modern Languages in the Secondary Modern School*. Report of a Committee. London: M.L.A., 1951. 38 pp.

STERN, H. H., ed. *Modern Languages in the Universities. A Guide to Courses*. London: Macmillan, 2nd edn., 1965. 364 pp.

UNESCO. *Second Language Teaching in Primary and Secondary Schools*. Paris: Education abstracts Vol. XIII, No. 3, 1961. 52 pp.

8 *Periodicals*

Modern Languages. The Journal of the Modern Language Association, 2 Manchester Square, London, W.1. Quarterly.

Audio-Visual Language Journal. Journal of Applied Linguistics and Language Teaching Technology. The organ of the Audio-Visual Language Association, 121 Gordon Road, South Woodford, London, E.18. Issued three times a year.

Le Français dans le Monde. Published by Hachette and Larousse, 79 Boulevard Saint-Germain, Paris 6e. Issued eight times a year.

Language Learning. A Journal of Applied Linguistics. North University Building, Ann Arbor, Michigan 48104, U.S.A. Issued twice a year.

The Modern Language Journal. Published by the National Federation of Modern Language Teachers Associations, 13149 Cannes Drive, St Louis, Missouri 63141, U.S.A. Issued eight times a year.

Index